450 ‹

A Brief Dictionary
of Hinduism

Formerly titled Ramakrishna Vedanta Wordbook

Nov/93

ISB-N-0-87481-048-5
22 340 $6.60
BRIEF DICT OF HINDU
        04/28/93

Vedanta
Press

ISBN 0-87481-048-5

Vedanta Press, Hollywood, California 90068

First edition published 1962.
5   6   7   8   9

Printed in the United States of America

PREFACE

The American or European student coming to Hinduism
for the first time encounters a number of words which are
for some new and forbidding: philosophical terms in
Sanskrit or Bengali; an array of difficult-sounding expres-
sions from Indian mythology and psychology; names of
unfamiliar places and people.

We have tried to meet the need for an inexpensive yet
accurate guide to these terms with the present small
volume. The book is primarily directed to students of
Vedanta, a branch of Hinduism, but it should easily meet
the needs of those who read most basic books on Hindu
philosophy.

One may ask: Why bother with Sanskrit or Bengali? Why
not simply use English equivalents? The answer is that this
cannot be done. The reason any foreign word comes into
a language is that it expresses an idea not easily expressed
with the words available in that language. Such is certainly
the case with the exact philosophical and religious terms
with which Indian religion abounds. There is the English
word *soul*, for example. If we were to use it in place of
Atman or *jiva*, gross misconceptions would result. *Atman*
and *jiva* have technical meanings that *soul* cannot approxi-
mate. And what English word can express the sense of say,
karma, which may mean a deed, the consequence of a deed,
the law of cause and effect operating in a moral world, or
the sum of consequences resulting from an individual's
actions in this and previous lives? For the sake of correct-

ness and clarity of expression, therefore, most Vedanta teachers and translators retain in the original a large number of Sanskrit and Bengali terms.

In addition to Sanskrit and Bengali philosophical and religious concepts, the student must cope with a sprinkling of terms related to Indian psychology, history, mythology and social custom. We have included some of these in this dictionary, as well as a few terms from Indian religions other than Hinduism—Buddhism, for instance. We have also defined several important English words such as *discrimination* and *non-attachment*, because the meaning of these to the Vedantist is specific and not always equivalent to Christian usage.

Since Vedanta philosophy owes its renaissance to Sri Ramakrishna, we have included as much information as possible about Sri Ramakrishna and the persons and places connected with him. In addition, the definitions of many of the philosophical concepts are given in terms of Sri Ramakrishna's personal religious experience.

We have not tried to include all the meanings of the words defined, but only those relevant to an understanding of Hinduism as taught in the Ramakrishna-Vedanta tradition. The reader should note that philosophical concepts shift in meaning depending on the particular system of thought in which they are used. Hindu deities may symbolize different concepts according to the sects in which they are worshiped.

The transliteration into English of Sanskrit and Bengali words presents many difficulties, due particularly to the fact that the Sanskrit and Bengali alphabets contain almost twice as many letters as the Roman alphabet, to express sounds often not found in English. We rejected the use of diacritical marks to express these additional sounds because of their scholarly, forbidding appearance.

Even if we were to use diacritical marks, exactitude in pronunciation still could not be achieved. There is a lack of agreement among Indian scholars as to the preferred form of many of the terms we have chosen to define. It is a matter of opinion whether, in certain words, to use *s*, or *v* or *w*; whether the Bengali *b* and *j* or the Sanskrit *v* and *y* are more desirable; and whether one should omit the *a* ending on a number of nouns as it customary in Bengal, or include the final *a* as is done in Sanskrit. In most cases we have followed the Sanskrit spelling, although Bengali or Hindi has guided us with certain words, as suggested by frequency of usage. Bearing the above-mentioned alternatives in mind, the reader occasionally will have to seek the word under either one or the other alphabetical entry before finding it.

We have settled arbitrarily for spellings and pronunciations which seem most natural and agreeable for the Westerner to use; there is no system of accentuation in Sanskrit and Bengali as there is in English. However, to further aid the student in approximating the pronunciation of Indian words, we have supplied, in phonetically spelled words, accent markings to indicate the syllables to be stressed.

A list of abbreviations used is given on page 9.

We are especially grateful for the invaluable guidance given by Swami Prabhavananda during the preparation of this manuscript.

The Publisher

KEY TO PRONUNCIATION
AND ABBREVIATIONS

a is sounded as in sof*a* (or as
   in b*o*x—Bengali usage)
ā is sounded as in st*a*r
e is sounded as in pr*ey*
 i is sounded as in s*i*t
 ī is sounded as in mach*i*ne
o is sounded as in s*o*
u is sounded as in p*u*ll
ū is sounded as in intr*u*de
ai is sounded as in *ai*sle
au is sounded as in n*ow*
 y is sounded as in *y*ou
 g is sounded as in *g*od
ng is sounded as in so*ng*
 ñ is sounded as in domi*ni*o*n*, maña*n*a
ch is sounded as in *ch*urch
 h after the following consonants
   is pronounced hard: bh as in
   ab*h*or; dh as in ad*h*ere; gh as
   in leg*h*orn; kh as in ink*h*orn.

ca.	*circa* (approximately)
cap.	capital letter
e.g.	*exempli gratia* (for example)
i.e.	*id est* (that is)
l.c.	lower case
lit.	literally
specif.	specifically

WORDBOOK

Abhedananda, Swami (a bhe′ dā′ nan da), Kali Prasad Chandra, 1866-1939, a monastic disciple of Sri Ramakrishna, whom Kali met in 1884. After his guru's passing away, Kali took up a wandering life, traveling widely throughout India and practicing intensive spiritual disciplines. In 1896, the Swami went to London to lecture on Vedanta; in 1897, to America, where he took charge of the Vedanta Society of New York. Upon his return to India, in 1921, he established the Ramakrishna Vedanta Society in Calcutta. Swami Abhedananda harmonized profound scholarship with a highly spiritual nature.

absorption. *See* SAMADHI.

achamana (ā′ cha ma na). Preliminary rite of the formal Hindu worship, or PUJA, in which the worshiper purifies himself by sipping and sprinkling water, and withdraws his mind from the sense world while making symbolic gestures.

acharya (ā′ chār′ ya). Spiritual teacher. The word is sometimes added to the name of a revered religious preceptor; *e.g.*, Shankaracharya.

Adbhutananda, Swami (ad bhu′ tā′ nan da), the first monastic disciple to come to Sri Ramakrishna, who called him Latu. Latu's early name was Rakhturam. Orphaned at the age of five, he became a servant of Ram Chandra DATTA, who brought him to Dakshineswar around 1880. Swami Adbhutananda was noted for his single-minded devotion and contemplative nature. Although illiterate, he demonstrated great wisdom and originality in answering questions on religious topics. He died in 1920.

adharma (a dhar′ ma). Unrighteousness, the absence of virtue. *See* DHARMA.

Adhyatma Ramayana (adh yāt′ ma   rā′ mā′ ya na). Lit., "spiritual interpretation of the life of Rama"; a subordinate, derivative RAMAYANA, interpreting the epic in terms of non-dualism and emphasizing the divine nature of Sri Rama and his close associates.

Advaitananda, Swami (ad vai tā′ nan da), Gopal Chandra Ghosh, 1823-1904, oldest monastic disciple of Sri Ramakrishna, known as the elder Gopal, or Gopal Senior. For some years a householder, employed in a shop in Calcutta, he began to frequent Dakshineswar after the death of his wife. He was one of 11 disciples to whom Sri Ramakrishna gave the ocher cloth of renunciation in 1886. Swami Advaitananda visited Indian places of pilgrimage at different periods. From 1899 until his death he stayed mainly at the Belur Math, where he managed various monastery activities. Advaitananda was renowned for his love of truth and his steadfastness in spiritual practices.

Advaita Vedanta (ad vai′ ta ve dān′ ta). Nondualistic VEDANTA. *See also* VEDANTA SCHOOLS OF THOUGHT.

Advaitist (ad vai′ tist). A follower of Advaita VEDANTA.

Agama (ā′ ga ma). 1. Scripture. 2. A Tantra, or any work inculcating the mystical worship of Shiva and Shakti.

agami karma (ā′ gā′ mi kar′ ma). The mental and physical acts performed by an individual in the present life, the fruits of which are to be reaped in the future. *See also* KARMA.

ahamkara (a ham′ kā′ ra). The ego-sense; a component of the mind which claims sense impressions for itself and establishes them as individual knowledge. *See also* COSMIC EVOLUTION.

ahimsa (a him′ sā). Nonviolence, abstention from harming any living being in thought, word, or deed.

ajna chakra (ā′ gñā′ chak′ ra). The sixth of seven yogic CENTERS OF CONSCIOUSNESS in the human body.

akasha (ā′ kā′ sha). Ether; the subtlest of the five elements. The substance supposed to fill and pervade the universe and to be the peculiar vehicle of life and sound. *See* COSMIC EVOLUTION.

Akhandananda, Swami (a khan′ dā′ nan da), Gangadhar Ghatak, 1866-1937, a monastic disciple of Sri Ramakrishna, who came to Dakshineswar in 1884. After his guru's death, Gangadhar joined the brotherhood at Baranagore. In 1887, he traveled on foot in the Himalayas, crossing into Tibet. Swami Akhandananda started his campaign against India's poverty and illiteracy in 1894, establishing schools and orphanages, and organizing the first flood and famine relief work of the Ramakrishna Math and Mission. His selfless service to the afflicted was an expression of his overflowing love of God. In 1934, the Swami became the third president of the Ramakrishna Order.

Alambazar (ā′ lam ba zār′). Site of the second monastery of Sri Ramakrishna's disciples, from 1891 to 1898, located between Baranagore and Dakshineswar, *ca.* three miles north of Calcutta.

Alvar (āl′ vār′). In Tamil, "he who rules (the world by his devotion to God)." The Alvars are Vaishnava saints of southern India.

amalaki (ā′ ma la kī′). A sacred tree of India *(Phyllanthus emblica). See also* PANCHAVATI.

anahata chakra (a nā′ ha ta chak′ ra). The fourth of seven yogic CENTERS OF CONSCIOUSNESS in the human body.

Anahata Shabda (a nā′ ha ta shab′ da). Lit., "unstruck sound," which may be heard in meditation at a certain stage of spiritual unfoldment. The word is applied to OM.

Ananda (ā′ nan da). 1. Philosophically speaking, pure

bliss or absolute joy; an aspect of Brahman. 2. *(l.c.)* In the monastic order of Shankara, the word constitutes the last part of the sannyas name; *e.g.,* Vivekananda ("whose bliss is in discrimination").

anandamaya-kosha (ā' nan da ma' ya ko' sha). The sheath of bliss. *See* KOSHA.

Anandamayi (ā' nan da ma yī'). God as the Blissful Mother.

annamaya-kosha (an' a ma' ya ko' sha). The physical sheath. *See* KOSHA.

Annapurna (an' na pūr' nā). A name of the Divine Mother, consort of Shiva. She is one of the two presiding deities of VARANASI.

antahkarana (an ta' ka ra na). Lit., "inner organ" or "internal instrument"; a word commonly used in Vedanta philosophy to denote the mind in a general way.

Antaryamin (an tar yā' min). God as the Inner Controller.

apara-vidya (a pa' rā vid' yā). Relative or lower knowledge, acquired through the intellect and the senses; knowledge of arts, sciences, scriptures, etc.—the opposite of PARA-VIDYA.

Aranyaka (ā' ran ya ka). *See* VEDA.

arati (ā' ra ti). A ceremonial waving of lights before a deity or holy person.

aratrika (ā' rā' tri ka). Same as ARATI.

arghya (argh' ya). A respectful offering to the deity in Hindu ritual worship, or PUJA, consisting of a flower, BEL leaf, sandalpaste, DURVA GRASS, and rice.

arhat (ar' hat). A Buddhist saint, enlightened by the attainment of NIRVANA.

Arjuna (ar' ju na). One of the five Pandava brothers and hero of the MAHABHARATA. Friend and disciple of Sri KRISHNA, in the Gita he is the representative spiritual aspirant through whom the Lord teaches mankind.

artha (ar′ ta). 1. Wealth. 2. Economic security; *see also* FOUR FRUITS.

Arya Samaj (ār′ ya   sa māj′). A religious and social reform movement of 19th-century India, founded by Swami Dayananda.

asana (ā′ sa na). 1. Place or mat on which the spiritual aspirant sits for meditation. According to the Gita, the place should be "firm, neither too high nor too low, and situated in a clean spot." Although traditionally it was covered by sacred grass, a deerskin, and a cloth, for the aspirant of today any convenient seat will do. 2. Position or posture of the body during meditation; the third of the eight limbs of raja yoga. Proper posture requires that the aspirant be seated with back, neck, and head held still and erect. Although some people prefer to sit cross-legged on the ground, this is by no means necessary. The important thing is to sit in an easy and natural position, which makes it possible to forget the body and concentrate the mind on God.

Ashoka (a sho′ ka). 1. Buddhist king of the 3rd century B.C. 2. (*l.c.*) *Saraca indica*, a tree of India with orange-scarlet flowers. *See also* PANCHAVATI.

ashrama (āsh′ ra ma), often ashram. 1. A center of religious study or meditation; a retreat, hermitage, or monastery. 2. Any one of the four stages into which man's life is divided according to Vedic teachings: celibate student life (brahmacharya); married householder life (garhasthya); the life of retirement and contemplation (vanaprastha); and monastic life (sannyas).

ashtami (ash′ ta mī′). The eighth day of either lunar fortnight.

Ashtavakra Samhita (ash tā′ vak ra   sam′ hi tā). A short treatise on Advaita Vedanta, ascribed to the sage Ashtavakra and presented in form of a dialogue.

ashvattha (ash vat′ ta). The holy fig tree *(Ficus religiosa).* *See also* PANCHAVATI.

Atharva Veda (a tar′ va ve′ da). *See* VEDA.

Atman (āt′ man). The Spirit or Self, the immanent aspect of the Godhead. *See also* JIVA; VEDANTA.

Aum. *See* OM.

austerity. The spiritual practice of conserving energy and directing it toward the realization of God. The Gita defines three kinds of true austerity: "Reverence for the DEVAs, the seers, the teachers, and the sages; straightforwardness, harmlessness, physical cleanliness, and sexual purity—these are the virtues whose practice is called austerity of the body. To speak without ever causing pain to another, to be truthful, to say always what is kind and beneficial, and to study the scriptures regularly—this practice is called austerity of speech. The practice of serenity, sympathy, meditation upon the Atman, withdrawal of the mind from sense-objects, and integrity of motive, is called austerity of the mind."

avatar (a va tār′), also avatara. A divine incarnation. According to Hindu belief, God as Vishnu descends into the finiteness of name and form in various ages to re-establish the forgotten truths of religion and to show mankind by his living example how to ascend to himself. The avatar is not born in consequence of past deeds and tendencies, like other embodied souls; his birth is the result of free choice. He is conscious of his divine mission throughout his life. He discovers new paths in the field of religion, which he adapts to the needs of the age. And he is able to transmit divine knowledge to his fellow beings by his mere touch, look, or wish. Among those widely accepted as avatars are Rama, Krishna, Buddha, Christ, and recently, Ramakrishna.

avidya (a vid′ yā). Ignorance. Philosophically speaking, avidya is individual ignorance, and MAYA is universal ignorance.

Ayodhya (a yodh′ yā). The capital of Sri RAMA's kingdom, on the river Sarayu in Uttar Pradesh, India.

Babu (bā′ bu). Mister, or esquire. The word is usually placed after the first name; *e.g.*, Girish Babu.

Baburam (bā′ bu rām′). Boyhood name of Swami PREMANANDA.

Baghbazar (bāg′ bā zār′). A section of Calcutta, where the UDBODHAN OFFICE and Balaram BOSE's house are located.

Balaram (ba′ la rām′). *See* BOSE.

Balarama (ba′ la rā′ ma). Brother of Sri Krishna. *See also* JAGANNATH.

banyan. Large Indian fig tree *(Ficus bengalensis)*. Its branches send out aerial roots which grow down to the soil and form additional trunks. *See also* PANCHAVATI.

Baranagore (ba rā′ na gar′). Site of the first monastery of Sri Ramakrishna's disciples, from 1886 to 1891, *ca.* two miles north of Calcutta, where the young monks devoted themselves to intensive spiritual disciplines.

bel (bel), or bilva. A tree *(Aegle marmelos)*, whose leaves are considered sacred and used in worship; also the fruit of the tree. *See also* PANCHAVATI.

Belur Math (be′ lur mat′). The monastery at Belur village, which constitutes the headquarters of the RAMAKRISHNA MATH AND MISSION. Consecrated in 1898, it is situated four miles north of Calcutta and fronts on the Ganges.

Benares. *See* VARANASI.

Bhagavad-Gita (bha′ ga vad gī′ tā), or Gita. Lit., "Song of God," it is the Gospel of Hinduism. Dated between the 5th and the 2nd centuries B.C., the Gita, which comprises 18 chapters, is a part of the MAHABHARATA. In the form of a dialogue between Sri KRISHNA, the divine incarnation, and his friend and disciple ARJUNA, it teaches how to achieve union with the supreme Reality through the paths of knowledge, devotion, selfless work, and meditation.

Bhagavan (bha′ ga vān). The Lord; the Personal God, endowed with six attributes: dominion, might, glory, splendor, wisdom, and renunciation.

Bhagavatam (bhā′ ga va tam), or Bhagavata Purana. The famous devotional Hindu scripture, attributed to Vyasa. The Bhagavatam illustrates religious truths with stories of ancient India's saints, seers, and kings. Dealing in part with the life of Sri Krishna, the divine incarnation, it is especially sacred to the VAISHNAVAS.

Bhagavata Purana (bhā′ ga va ta pu rā′ na). Same as BHAGAVATAM.

Bhagavati (bha′ ga va tī). Goddess; a name of the Divine Mother.

Bhairava (bhai′ ra va). A name of Shiva; but more usually, a divine attendant of Shiva.

Bhairavi (bhai′ ra vī). 1. A nun of the Tantric sect. 2. The BHAIRAVI BRAHMANI.

Bhairavi Brahmani (bhai′ ra vī brā′ ma nī), also known as the Brahmani or the Bhairavi. A wandering nun, whose name was Yogeshvari, and who, in 1861, initiated Sri Ramakrishna into the disciplines of TANTRA. She was the first to proclaim him an avatar.

bhajan (bha′ jan). Worship of God with singing.

bhakta (bhak′ ta). A devotee of God.

bhakti (bhak′ ti). Devotion to God.

bhakti yoga (bhak′ ti yo′ ga). The path of devotion; one of the four main yogas, or paths to union with God. After cultivating intense love for one of the many aspects of God as a personal being—often as a divine incarnation— the worshiper ultimately merges his own ego in his CHOSEN IDEAL.

Bhakti yoga is the most natural path to God-realization. The BHAKTA has not to suppress his emotions; he intensifies them and directs them to God. The majority of believers in all the great religions of the world are fundamentally followers of this path. The five chief BHAVAS of the devotee toward his Chosen Ideal are 1. shanta (the attitude of peace and serenity), in which God is felt near but no definite relationship has been established between him and the worshiper; 2. dasya (the attitude of servant toward Master and child toward Parent and Protector); 3. sakhya (the attitude of friend toward Friend); 4. vatsalya (the attitude of parent toward Child); and 5. madhura (the attitude of wife or lover toward Husband or Beloved). In bhakti yoga, there are various stages: 1. bhakti (devotion); 2. bhava (matured bhakti—a state of ecstasy); 3. prema (a state in which the devotee forgets the world and his own body); 4. mahabhava (the highest manifestation of divine love, of which RADHA is considered an embodiment). Only AVATARS and ISHVARAKOTIS can transcend the stage of bhava.

Bharata (bha′ ra ta). 1. A holy man and former king, mentioned in the Bhagavatam. 2. A brother of Sri Rama.

Bharata (bhā′ ra ta). A name of India (in honor of King Bharata).

bhashya (bhāsh′ ya). A commentary.

Bhaskara (bhās′ ka ra). An Indian philosopher, said to have lived in the early part of the 9th century A.D. He expounded the philosophy of Bhedabheda, the doctrine of identity in difference, which teaches that individual souls are parts of the supreme Reality—neither absolutely identical with Brahman nor absolutely different from him. Bhaskara believed that complete union with Brahman is possible only after the death of the body.

bhava (bhā′ va). State of being, feeling, emotion; an attitude assumed toward God in BHAKTI YOGA; ecstasy (matured bhakti).

bhava-mukha (bhā′ va mu′ kha). A high state of spiritual awareness, between the Relative and the Absolute. Technically speaking, in bhava-mukha the spiritual aspirant's mind moves between the ajna chakra and sahasrara. *See* CENTERS OF CONSCIOUSNESS.

bhava samadhi (bhā′ va sa mā′ dhi). A state of ecstasy, attained by following the path of devotion. In this state, a trace of ego remains in the worshiper, enabling him to enjoy God and his divine play—in the words of Sri Ramakrishna, "to taste sugar rather than become sugar."

Bhavatarini (bha′ va tā′ ri nī). Redeemer of the Universe; the Divine Mother KALI, worshiped under this name at the DAKSHINESWAR temple.

bhiksha (bhik′ shā). Alms.

bhikshu (bhik′ shu). 1. A mendicant. 2. Specif., Buddhist monk (Buddhist spelling: bhikku).

bhoga (bho′ ga). 1. Enjoyment of sense objects. 2. Food offered to a deity.

bija mantra (bī′ ja man′ tra). Lit., "seed word"; the letter or syllable of the MANTRA, in which the essence of a particular aspect of God is concentrated in the form of a sound-symbol. Such sound-symbols, evolved out of the spiritual experiences of saints, are charged with the living power of God when received from a qualified GURU.

bilva (bil′ va). Same as BEL.

bodhisattva (bo′ dhi sat′ va). In Mahayana Buddhism, an advanced soul in the last stage before attaining complete enlightenment, or Buddhahood. The bodhisattva postpones his final liberation voluntarily to help mankind.

bodhi tree (bo′ dhi), or bo tree. The holy fig tree *(Ficus religiosa);* specif. *(cap.),* the sacred tree at Buddh-Gaya, under which Gautama Buddha attained NIRVANA.

Bose, Balaram (bos). A pious householder-disciple of Sri Ramakrishna—descendant of a wealthy Vaishnava family—whose home in Calcutta Sri Ramakrishna frequently visited.

bo tree. Same as BODHI TREE.

Brahma (bra′ mā). God in the aspect of Creator of the Universe, one of the Hindu Trinity. Brahma is usually represented with four faces and four arms, holding among other symbols the VEDA and a rosary. *See also* ISHVARA.

brahmachari (bra′ ma chā′ rī). 1. A spiritual aspirant who has taken the first monastic vows. 2. An individual devoted to continence and other religious practices in observance of the first of the four stages of life according to Vedic teachings. *See also* ASHRAMA.

brahmacharini (bra′ ma chā′ ri nī). Feminine form of BRAHMACHARI.

brahmacharya (bra′ ma char′ ya). 1. Continence in thought, word, and deed. 2. Initiation in which the religious aspirant takes the first monastic vows; also the status of one who has taken the vows. (In the Ramakrishna Order a minimum period of five years as a probationer is obligatory before the vows of brahmacharya are conferred.) 3. The celibate student stage, the first of the four stages into which the life of an individual is divided according to Vedic teachings. In this stage a boy lives in the company of his teacher, receiving secular as well as religious instruction, and is trained in the practice of continence and other virtues. *See also* ASHRAMA.

Brahmajnana (bra′ ma gñyā′ na). The transcendental knowledge of Brahman.

Brahmaloka (bra′ ma lo′ ka). A heaven, or plane of existence, where spiritually evolved souls go after death to live in divine communion.

Brahman (bra′ man). The impersonal absolute Existence

or Godhead, the all-pervading transcendental Reality of VE-
DANTA philosophy. *See also* MAYA.

Brahmana (brā′ ma na). *See* VEDA.

Brahmananda, Swami (bra′ mā′ nan da), Rakhal Chandra
Ghosh, 1863-1922, a monastic disciple of Sri Ramakrishna
whom the latter regarded as his spiritual son as well as an
ISHVARAKOTI. Rakhal came to Dakshineswar in 1881, where
Sri Ramakrishna trained him in many kinds of spiritual disciplines. Called Raja ("the King") by his brother-disciples,
he later became familiarly known to devotees as Maharaj.
After Sri Ramakrishna's passing away, he was put in charge of
the monastery at Baranagore. Subsequently he made pilgrimages in northern India, joining his brother monks again in
1894, at Alambazar. In 1897, Maharaj became president of
Belur Math, and in 1900, president of the Ramakrishna Math
and Mission. In this capacity he toured northern and southern India, East Bengal and Assam, giving existing Ramakrishna
centers fresh impetus and starting new ones. Maharaj was a
great reservoir of spiritual power, in whose presence the life
and character of many became transformed.

Brahmani (brā′ ma nī). 1. (l.c.) A brahmin woman. 2.
The BHAIRAVI BRAHMANI.

Brahma Sutras (bra′ ma   sū′ tras). Same as VEDANTA
SUTRAS.

Brahmavidya (bra′ ma vid′ yā). Same as BRAHMAJNANA.

brahmin (brā′ min). *See* CASTE.

Brahmo Samaj (brā′ mo   sa māj′). A religious and social
reform movement of 19th-century India, dedicated to the
"worship and adoration of the Eternal, the Unsearchable, the
Immutable Being, who is the Author and Preserver of the
Universe." Founded by Raja Rammohan Roy and organized
by Devendranath Tagore, its membership was open to all regardless of creed, caste, color, and country. Keshab Chandra

SEN was its most famous leader.

breathing exercises. *See* PRANAYAMA.

Brindavan (brin' dā' van). A town on the banks of the river Jamuna, in Uttar Pradesh, associated with the childhood of Sri Krishna.

Buddha (bud' dha). Lit., "the Enlightened One." 1. The word refers specif. to Gautama Buddha, *ca.* 567-483 B.C. Born as Prince Siddhartha, he renounced the world to become one of the great spiritual teachers of all time, and the founder of BUDDHISM. 2. The generic term may refer to any being who has reached NIRVANA, and bears certain physical marks characteristic of this attainment.

Buddh-Gaya (buddh' ga yā). A place, seven miles south of Gaya, in Bihar State, where Buddha attained NIRVANA.

buddhi (bud' dhi). The discriminative faculty in the individual, which classifies sense impressions. *See also* COSMIC EVOLUTION.

Buddhism. One of the great religions of the world, founded by Gautama Buddha and based on the following doctrines. 1. The Four Noble Truths: that there is suffering; that there is a cause of suffering; that suffering can be overcome; and that there is a way of peace. 2. Nirvana: The world of mind and matter is in a state of constant flux. To withdraw the mind from the flux and to attain NIRVANA—the state of enlightenment and perfection—is to free oneself from suffering and rebirth. 3. The Eightfold Path: right view, right aspiration, right speech, right conduct, right livelihood, right effort, right mindfulness, and right contemplation. The two main schools of Buddhism are Hinayana (the Narrow Way) and Mahayana (the Great Way). The ideal of Hinayana is arhathood, the achievement of personal sanctity through ascetic seclusion. Mahayana, popularizing the teachings of the founder, propounds worship of Gautama Buddha as a divine incarnation and exalts the BODHISATTVA.

burning-ghat. *See* GHAT.

calendar, Bengali. The lunar months of the Bengali year are: Vaishakh (middle of April to middle of May), Jyaishtha (middle of May to middle of June), Ashard (middle of June to middle of July), Shravan (middle of July to middle of August), Bhadra (middle of August to middle of September), Ashvin (middle of September to middle of October), Kartik (middle of October to middle of November), Agrahayan (middle of November to middle of December), Paush (middle of December to middle of January), Magh (middle of January to middle of February), Phalgun (middle of February to middle of March), Chaitra (middle of March to middle of April).

caste. A social system established in India by the Aryans, probably at first determined by a man's occupation. With the passing of centuries caste became hereditary and was surrounded by many restrictions designed to prevent caste-mixture. Those belonging to the lowest stratum of Hindu society, called untouchables, were considered outside the caste system. They were originally excluded for their primitive and outlandish socio-religious customs, a practice which later became hereditary. In the footsteps of Hindu reformers of the 19th century, India's government of today is following the policy of abolishing caste by degrees. As described in the Gita, the idea of caste refers to a natural order—determined by a man's KARMA and predominating GUNA. The four main castes are: 1. the brahmin caste (priests, pandits, philosophers, religious leaders); the kshatriya caste (politicians, military men, persons of royal descent—an upper division within this caste is known as kayastha in northern India and Bengal); the vaishya caste (caste of providers, which includes merchants, farmers, and artisans); and the shudra caste (laborers and servants). In this sense, the castes are necessary components of human society. The Gita teaches that by performing his caste duty as worship of God, each man can transcend caste and all other karmic limitations, and reach the spiritual perfection which is his birthright.

causal body. The anandamaya-KOSHA.

centers of consciousness. In the human body, along the central spinal canal (called SUSHUMNA) six main chakras (centers of consciousness) are located. These chakras, and a seventh center in the cerebrum, are sometimes called "lotuses" in yogic language because they are said to open like lotus blossoms and resemble them in shape. The centers, which are spiritual, parallel various nerve-plexuses described in anatomy. They are said to have certain colors and numbers of petals. When the KUNDALINI becomes awakened and travels through the centers, it produces various spiritual experiences and degrees of illumination. Sri Ramakrishna's description of the centers follows: "When the mind is attached to worldliness, consciousness dwells in the three lower centers, the plexus sacro-coccygeal (muladhara), sacral (svadhishthana), and solar (manipura). Then there are in it no high ideals or pure thoughts. It remains immersed in lust and greed. The fourth center of consciousness (anahata) is in the region of the heart. Spiritual awakening comes when the mind rises to this center. At this stage man has a spiritual vision of the Divine Light and is struck with wonder at its beauty and glory. His mind then no longer runs after worldly pleasures. The region of the throat is the fifth center of consciousness (vishuddha). When the mind rises to this center, man becomes free from nescience and ignorance. He then talks only on subjects relating to God. . . . The sixth center (ajna) is between the eyebrows. When the mind rises to this center, man becomes merged in divine consciousness. There is still left in him, however, the consciousness of a separate ego. Seeing the beatific vision of God, he becomes mad with joy and longs to come closer to him and be united with him. But he cannot, for there is still the ego which stands between them. . . . The center in the brain (SA-HASRARA) is the seventh center. When one rises to this plane there is samadhi. That is the transcendental consciousness, in which one realizes his oneness with God."

chadar (chā′ dar). A long piece of cloth worn on the upper part of the body, often draped as a shawl. 1. A traditional garment of the orthodox male Hindu. 2. A component of the monastic dress in the Ramakrishna Order. 3. In the West, lay and monastic Vedantists often use the chadar during meditation, for purposes of warmth and concealment of the rosary.

Chaitanya (chai′ tan ya), also known as Nimai, Gaur, Gauranga, and Krishna Chaitanya. A great saint and spiritual teacher, born in 1485, in Navadvip, Bengal, who later lived in Orissa. A brilliant scholar, he suddenly renounced the world and became an ardent devotee of Sri Krishna, of whom (according to Bengal Vaishnavas) he was a partial incarnation. His ecstatic love of God embraced sinners and saints, regardless of caste and creed. Sri Chaitanya stressed BHAKTI YOGA as a way to God-realization with special emphasis on JAPA as a spiritual practice.

Chaitanya (chai′ tan ya). Spiritual or awakened consciousness. In the Ramakrishna Order, the word Chaitanya is added to the names of brahmacharis; *e.g.*, Bhakti Chaitanya ("whose consciousness is filled with devotion").

chakra (chak′ ra). *See* CENTERS OF CONSCIOUSNESS.

chamar (chā′ mar). A fan made of the bushy tail of the chamari, or yak, used in Hindu ritual worship.

chana (chā′ nā). A soft cheese made from curdled milk. Sweets or a curry may be prepared from it.

Chandi (chan′ dī). *The Devi Mahatmyam.* Puranic scripture praising the Divine Mother.

Chandra Devi (chan' drā   de' vī). Chandramani, 1791-1876, wife of Khudiram Chattopadhyaya and mother of Sri Ramakrishna.

chapati (cha pā' tī). The Indian counterpart of bread, made from whole-wheat flour. It resembles the Mexican tortilla in size and shape.

Charvaka (chār' vā ka). An Indian philosopher who taught a doctrine of scepticism and materialism.

Chit (chit). Philosophically speaking, pure unitary contentless Consciousness—unlike ordinary consciousness which has an object as its content; an aspect of Brahman.

chitta (chit' ta). In Yoga terminology, the mind-stuff, whose three components are MANAS, BUDDHI, and AHAMKARA.

Chosen Ideal (Ishta, in Sanskrit). The aspect of the Godhead selected by a spiritual aspirant, or by his GURU for him. Through meditation on his Chosen Ideal, the aspirant gradually attains concentration of mind, love of God, and ultimately illumination. *See also* MANTRA.

cosmic evolution. According to SANKHYA cosmology, the universe is an evolution of PRAKRITI (primordial nature). Through its proximity to PURUSHA (Pure Consciousness, or Spirit), the active but insentient prakriti produces the following cosmic principles: first mahat, cosmic intelligence. Then come AHAMKARA (the ego-sense); BUDDHI (the discriminative faculty of the individual); and MANAS (the recording faculty of the mind). There also evolve the five organs of perception (sight, hearing, smell, taste, touch); the five organs of action (tongue, hands, feet, the organs of excretion and generation); and the five tanmatras—subtle principles which, by combining and recombining, produce the five gross elements: ether (akasha), air, fire, water, earth. Sankhya cosmology, followed by YOGA, is also largely accepted by VE-

DANTA. The main difference is that Sankhya and Yoga postulate two ultimate realities (Purusha and prakriti), whereas Vedanta postulates one Absolute, which it calls Brahman. Vedanta regards prakriti (also called maya) as Brahman's power—dependent upon and non-separate from Brahman. For the purpose of creating, preserving, and dissolving the universe, Brahman united with his maya manifests as the Personal God, or Ishvara.

Cossipore. *See* KASHIPUR.

Dakshineswar (dak' shi nesh' war). A village on the Ganges (*ca.* five miles north of Calcutta, where, in the 1850's, the Rani RASMANI built a group of temples: the Kali temple, 12 small Shiva temples, and the RADHAKANTA temple. Just north of the northernmost Shiva temple is the room which Sri Ramakrishna occupied for a considerable part of his life.

dal (dāl). Lentils; also the gravy made from lentils and spices.

darshan (dar' shan). Lit., "seeing, experiencing"; paying respects to a holy place or person by a ceremonial visit; also the blessing or purification felt in the presence of holiness.

darshana (dar' sha na). Philosophy. The six darshanas (systems of orthodox Hindu philosophy) are: the NYAYA of Gotama, the VAISHESHIKA of Kanada, the SANKHYA of Kapila, the YOGA of Patanjali, the PURVA MIMAMSA of Jaimini, and the Vedanta (or UTTARA MIMAMSA) of Vyasa.

Dasharatha (da' sha ra ta). The father of Sri Rama.

dasya (dās' ya). *See* BHAKTI YOGA.

Datta, Ram Chandra (dat' ta). The first householder-disciple to come to Sri Ramakrishna (in 1879), and the first disciple to proclaim the Master a divine incarnation.

deva (de' va). A god, or the male form of a semi-divine being. The word *(cap.)* may be added to the name of a God-man to connote reverence; *e.g.*, Chaitanya Deva.

Devaki (de' va kī). The mother of Sri Krishna.

devi (de' vī). Lit., "goddess"; the word may refer to any female deity of Hinduism. The word *(cap.)* often follows the name of a goddess, *e.g.*, Lakshmi Devi; it is also added to the first names of Indian ladies to connote respect.

Dhammapada (dham' ma pa da). The famous Buddhist text on spiritual life, ascribed to Gautama Buddha.

dharana (dhā' ra nā). Concentration; the sixth of the eight limbs of raja yoga, defined by Patanjali as "holding the mind within a center of spiritual consciousness in the body or fixing it on a divine form either within the body or outside it."

dharma (dhar' ma). Lit., "that which holds your true nature"; the word may denote merit, morality, righteousness, truth, religious duty, or the way of life which a man's nature imposes upon him. It is also the first of the FOUR FRUITS of human life. In Buddhism, dharma (spelled dhamma) also means the Buddhist doctrine.

dhoti (dho' ti). A male Hindu's wearing-cloth: a long piece of material draped around the waist.

Dhruva (dhru' va). A boy devotee of Vishnu, mentioned in the Bhagavatam.

dhuni (dhū' ni). A fire lighted by wandering monks, beside which they meditate and sleep.

dhyana (dhyā' na). Meditation, or deepened concentration. Dhyana is the seventh of the eight limbs of raja yoga, defined by Patanjali as "an unbroken flow of thought toward the object of concentration." The process is often compared to pouring oil from one vessel to another in a steady stream. (The Japanese word *Zen* owes its origin to the Sanskrit *dhyana*.)

diksha (dīk' shā). INITIATION of an aspirant into spiritual life by a GURU.

disciple. A spiritual aspirant who accepts a GURU as his guide in religious life. *See also* INITIATION; MANTRA.

discrimination. In Vedanta terminology, knowledge of what is eternal and what is noneternal; and devotion to the eternal, which is God. Shankara mentions discrimination as the first qualification of the spiritual aspirant, defining it as "the firm conviction that Brahman alone is real and the universe unreal."

Divine Mother. The dynamic aspect of the Godhead, which is usually represented in female form. The Mother appears under many different names as the divine consort of Brahma, Vishnu, or Shiva. According to the Vaishnavas and Shaivas, she is not independent of the father aspect of the Godhead. *See also* SHAKTI.

Durga (dur′ gā). Lit., "the Incomprehensible One"; a name of the DIVINE MOTHER, consort of Shiva. Her ten-armed form, with a lion as mount, symbolizes her great power. She destroys the demon of ignorance while blessing with divine love and knowledge those who yearn for God-realization.

Durga puja (dur′ gā pū′ jā). The annual worship of DURGA in autumn, for which a new image of the deity is made each year. In Bengal, the five-day celebration begins with a supplication, petitioning Durga to come to earth from her heavenly home, the main ritual worships taking place on the following three days. On the last day (VIJAYA DAY) the image is immersed in a river or ocean.

durva grass (dūr′ vā). Three-pointed sacred grass, prepared for use in the Hindu ritual worship, or PUJA, by separating the outer from the inner blades. This act symbolizes the spiritual aspirant's effort to separate the Atman from the body in his consciousness.

dvaita (dvai′ ta). The philosophy of dualism, in which man, as a creature, and God, as the Creator, are considered separate from each other. *See* VEDANTA SCHOOLS OF THOUGHT.

Dwapara yuga (dwā′ pa ra yu′ ga). The third of the four world periods, which is said to comprise 864,000 years. *See* YUGA.

Dwaraka (dwā′ ra kā). One of the principal holy places of India, situated at its farthest western point. The deity worshiped in its famous temple is Sri Krishna.

ego. "I"-consciousness; consciousness of a separate individuality from Atman, or God. Sri Ramakrishna used to distinguish between two kinds of ego, "unripe" and "ripe." The unripe ego is arrogant and self-centered—worldly. The ripe ego, which considers itself a child, servant, or devotee of God, cannot injure anyone; it is retained by illumined souls, after they come down from the transcendental to the ordinary plane of consciousness, to teach spirituality to others. The ripe ego is also known as the ego of knowledge or devotion.

ekadashi (e kā′ da shī). The eleventh day after the new or full moon, which orthodox Hindus observe by worship, meditation, and fasting.

enlightenment. *See* NIRVANA.

faith. According to Shankara's *Crest-Jewel of Discrimination*, this virtue is a prerequisite for the seeker after the knowledge of Brahman. Shankara says: "A firm conviction, based upon intellectual understanding, that the teachings of the scriptures and of one's master are true—this is called by the sages the faith that leads to realization of the Reality."

four fruits or goals of human life: dharma (morality, religious duty); artha (economic security); kama (fulfillment of legitimate desires); and MOKSHA.

Gadadhar (ga dā′ dhar). Lit., "Wielder of the Mace"; a name of Vishnu, and childhood name of Sri Ramakrishna.

Ganapati (ga′ na pa ti). A name of GANESHA.

Ganesha (ga ne′ sha), also Ganapati. The son of Shiva and Parvati, represented with an elephant's head. Ganesha is the god of wisdom and remover of obstacles, who grants success in spiritual as well as worldly life. He is worshiped at the beginning of all ten- and sixteen-item PUJAS.

Ganga (gang' gā). Sanskrit and Bengali word for Ganges, the Indian river which rises in the Himalayas and flows into the Bay of Bengal. It is considered as sacred by Hindus as the Jordan is held to be by Christians.

Gangadhar (gang' gā dhar). Boyhood name of Swami AKHANDANANDA.

garhasthya (gār' hast ya). Married householder life. *See also* ASHRAMA.

Gaudapada (gau' da pā' da). Vedantic philosopher and first historic expounder of nondualism, who lived sometime before the 8th century, A.D. He wrote the famous Karika—a treatise on the Mandukya Upanishad—upon which Shankara wrote a commentary.

Gaur (gaur), or Gauranga. *See* Sri CHAITANYA.

Gauri (gau' rī). A name of the Divine Mother, consort of Shiva.

Gauri Ma (gau' rī mā'). Mridani, *ca.* 1857-1938, a woman disciple of Sri Ramakrishna, who devoted her life to strenuous spiritual practice and to the cause of women in Bengal.

Gaya (ga' yā). A place of pilgrimage in Bihar, northern India. Its famous temple is dedicated to Vishnupada (the lotus-feet of Vishnu).

Gayatri (gā' ya trī). 1. The sacred Vedic MANTRA: "May we meditate on the effulgent Light of him who is worshipful, and who has given birth to all worlds. May he direct the rays of our intelligence toward the path of good." Once the orthodox Hindu boy has gone through the UPANAYANA ceremony, he recites this verse daily. 2. The presiding deity of the Gayatri mantra.

gerua (ge' ru ā). 1. the ocher color, symbol of renunciation. 2. The ocher cloth of SANNYASINS and SANNYASINIS.

ghat (ghāt). A place, often with steps, where people descend to a river or lake, usually for bathing. Burning-ghats are reserved for cremation, so that the funeral party may have access to a body of water for purification and for disposal of ashes.

ghee (ghī). Butter which has been clarified by boiling. It is used in preparing wicks for ARATI lights, as an ingredient in some PUJA offerings, and in Hindu cooking.

Ghosh, Girish Chandra (ghosh), 1844-1912, a householder-disciple of Sri Ramakrishna. Girish was a brilliant Bengali playwright, actor, director, and producer. His life, which he had given to worldly enjoyments, was completely transformed by his guru's influence; and Girish became an example of faith in and self-surrender to God.

Girish (gi rīsh'). *See* GHOSH.

Gita (gī' tā). Same as BHAGAVAD-GITA.

Golap Ma (go lāp' mā'). Golapsundari, a woman disciple of Sri Ramakrishna and close companion of Sri SARADA DEVI.

gopa (go' pa). A cowherd boy of Brindavan. The gopas were playmates and devotees of Sri Krishna.

Gopal Sr. (go' pāl). See Swami ADVAITANANDA.

Gopala (go' pā la). Name of Baby KRISHNA; lit., "he who preserves earth and animals."

Gopaler Ma (go' pā ler mā'), or GOPALA's Mother. Aghoremani Devi, a woman disciple of Sri Ramakrishna, who came to Dakshineswar in 1884. She was ecstatically devoted to the Lord as Baby Krishna, and considered Sri Ramakrishna to be the embodiment of her Chosen Ideal.

gopi (go' pī). A milkmaid of Brindavan. The gopis were companions and devotees of Sri Krishna. Examples of the most intense divine love, they were considered by Sri Ramakrishna to have been RISHIS in an earlier incarnation.

goswami (go' swā mī). A Vaishnava priest. The goswamis are brahmins, descendants of NITYANANDA.

Govinda (go vin' da). Lit., "by whom heaven is obtained"; a name of Sri Krishna.

guna (gu' na). Any one of three types of energies: sattva, rajas, and tamas. The three gunas, which constitute PRA-KRITI, make up the universe of mind and matter. When the gunas are in perfect balance, there is no creation, expression, or manifestation. When the balance is disturbed, creation occurs. (*See* COSMIC EVOLUTION.) In the physical world, sattva embodies what is pure and fine (*e.g.*, sunlight); rajas embodies the active principle (an erupting volcano); and tamas embodies solidity and resistance (a block of granite). From the standpoint of evolution, sattva is the essence of the form to be realized; tamas is the obstacle to its realization; and rajas is the power by which the obstacle is removed. In the mind of man, sattva expresses itself as calmness and purity; rajas as activity, passion, and restlessness; tamas as laziness, inertia, stupidity. Man's mood and character vary according to the predominating guna. The spiritual aspirant must overcome tamas by rajas, and rajas by sattva. In order to realize the Atman, or Purusha, sattva must also be transcended.

Gupta, Mahendranath (gup' ta), 1854-1932, a householder-disciple of Sri Ramakrishna. Popularly known as "M." or Master Mahashay, he was a school principal, versed in Western philosophy, who came to Dakshineswar in 1882. From his Bengali diaries, M. compiled the Sri Sri Ramakrishna Kathamrita (translated as The Gospel of Sri Ramakrishna), in which he has left an almost stenographic record of many of his master's conversations. M.'s humility and love of God inspired many young people to dedicate themselves to a spiritual life.

guru (gu' ru). A spiritual teacher. A qualified guru is, ideally, an illumined soul, or well advanced on the religious path. Swami Vivekananda says that a guru must know the spirit of the scriptures; he must be sinless; and he must teach selflessly, without desire for name, fame, or wealth. A competent guru assumes responsibility for the spiritual life of his disciple and leads him to salvation. *See also* INITIATION; MANTRA.

gurubhai (gu′ ru bhāi′). A brother-disciple; any male person initiated by the same spiritual teacher. (Feminine: gurubhagini.)

Guru Maharaj (gu′ ru ma′ hā rāj). Lit., "great teacher"; a respectful way of referring to the guru. Among Ramakrishna devotees, the word is reserved for Sri Ramakrishna.

Haladhari (ha′ la dhā rī). A cousin of Sri Ramakrishna, who served as a priest in one of the Dakshineswar temples.

halwa (hāl′ wā). An Indian dessert made from farina.

Hanuman (ha′ nu mān), or Mahavir. Leader of Sri RAMA's army and a hero of the Ramayana. Hanuman is revered in India as the ideal devotee because of his ecstatic love for Sri Rama. *See also* VEDANTA SCHOOLS OF THOUGHT.

Hara (ha′ ra). A name of Shiva.

Hari (ha′ ri). 1. A name of the Lord as Vishnu-Krishna. 2. Pre-monastic name of Swami TURIYANANDA.

Hari bol (ha′ ri bol′). An expression of the Vaishnavas, meaning "chant the Lord's name."

Hari Om (ha′ ri om′). Sacred syllables, used to invoke the presence of God.

Hari Prasanna (ha′ ri pra san′ na). Pre-monastic name of Swami VIJNANANANDA.

hatha yoga (ha′ ta yo′ ga). A system of physical exercises. Its principal object being physical health, it is much concerned with postures of the body and with PRANAYAMA. Hatha yoga should not be confused with systems of yoga the purpose of which is the attainment of spiritual perfection.

Hiranyagarbha (hi ran' ya gar' bha). The first manifestation of Brahman with attributes, the name is applied to Brahma, the Creator.

Holy Mother. *See* SARADA DEVI.

homa (ho' ma). A ceremony, dating from Vedic times, in which oblations are offered into a fire built according to scriptural injunctions. The fire is considered to be the visible manifestation of the deity worshiped. The homa is a ritual of inner purification, at the end of which the devotee makes a mental offering to the deity of all his thoughts, words, actions, and their fruits.

Hooghly (hug' lī). 1. The most westerly channel of the Ganges river in its delta. 2. A town by that name.

Hriday (hri' dai). A nephew of Sri Ramakrishna, also known as Hride or Hridu, born in 1829. He came to Dakshineswar in 1855, to serve as his uncle's attendant, and stayed with him for nearly 25 years.

ida (i dā'). A column of sensory and motor fibers on the left side of the spinal cord. *See* SUSHUMNA.

illumination. *See* NIRVANA.

immortality. A state of being, beyond time, space, and causation. Immortality is therefore not a continuity of existence in time, but a superconscious state in which the individual soul realizes its identity with the Godhead.

Indra (in' dra). A Vedic deity, known as king of the gods.

indriya (in' dri ya). The sense organs; they consist of five organs of perception (sight, hearing, smell, taste, touch), five organs of action (tongue, hands, feet, the organs of excretion and generation), and the mind.

initiation. The ceremony (diksha, in Sanskrit) which symbolizes the beginning of spiritual life. During initiation the GURU gives his disciple specific instructions in spiritual practices—more particularly a MANTRA. The usual form of diksha is mantri—with the guru whispering the mantra into the ear of the disciple. Two other forms of diksha, shambhavi and shakti, are effected by the mere wish, look, or touch of the guru, and produce immediate illumination in the disciple. Shambhavi and shakti initiation can only be given by AVATARS or ISHVARAKOTIS. Initiation may also refer to ceremonies of acceptance into monastic life—either BRAHMACHARYA or SAN-NYAS.

Ishana (ī′ shā na). A name of Shiva.

Ishta (ish′ ta). The CHOSEN IDEAL.

Ishvara (īsh′ va ra). Brahman united with maya, his power; God with attributes; the Personal God. According to Swami Vivekananda, Ishvara is "the highest possible reading of the Absolute by the human mind." Ishvara's three aspects with respect to the universe (known as the Hindu Trinity) have been personified as Brahma (the Creator), Vishnu (the Preserver), and Shiva (the Dissolver).

Ishvarakoti (īsh′ va ra ko′ ti). One belonging to a class of eternally free and perfect souls, born on earth for the good of mankind. According to Sri Ramakrishna, an Ishvarakoti has at least some of the characteristics of an AVATAR.

Jagadamba (ja′ ga dam bā). Lit., "Mother of the Universe"; a name of the Divine Mother, consort of Shiva.

Jagaddhatri (ja′ gad dhā′ trī). Lit., "Preserver of the Universe"; a name of the Divine Mother, consort of Shiva.

Jagannath (ja′ gan nāt). Lit., "Lord of the Universe." 1. A name of Vishnu. 2. The famous temple at PURI where this aspect of Vishnu is worshiped. The image in this temple— said by some historians to have been Buddhist, Shaivite, and Vaishnavite successively—has long been identified as Sri Krishna, flanked on either side by his sister Subhadra and his brother Balarama.

jai (jai), or jaya. A word meaning "hail," "victory to," or "glory to." It is often chanted aloud by devotees, singly or in groups, in such combinations as: "Jai Sri Guru Maharajji ki jai" ("Hail to the Great Guru, hail"—applied to Sri Ramakrishna by his followers); "Jaya Sri Ramakrishna"; or "Jaya Sri Durga."

Jain (jain). A follower of JAINISM.

Jainism (jain′ ism). An Indian religion which teaches the potential divinity of every soul, and worship of perfected souls as the Supreme Spirit. Liberation is achieved through right faith, right knowledge, and right conduct (with special emphasis on noninjury of any living being). Mahavira, a contemporary of Buddha, is one of the most famous teachers of Jainism.

Jamuna (ja′ mu nā), also Jumna, or Yamuna. A sacred river of northern India.

Janaka (ja′ na ka). A famous king and the father of SITA. He was a knower of Brahman as well as ruler of his kingdom (ancient Videha). Sri Ramakrishna said that Janaka combined YOGA and BHOGA.

Janaki (jā′ na kī). A name of SITA.

japa (ja′ pa), also japam. The practice of repeating one of God's names—usually one's own MANTRA. A rosary may be used to facilitate counting a required amount.

jatra (jāt′ rā). Country theater; drama, often religious, commonly performed in open-air theaters in Bengal villages.

jaya (ja′ ya). Same as JAI.

Jayrambati (jai′ rām bā′ tī). The village in Bankura district, West Bengal, where Sri SARADA DEVI was born.

jiva (jī′ va). The individual soul or human self. Philosophically speaking, jiva is the ATMAN identified with its coverings —body, mind, senses, etc. Ignorant of its divinity, it experiences birth and death, pleasure and pain.

jivanmukta (jī′ van muk′ ta). One who has attained JI-

VANMUKTI.

jivanmukti (jī' van muk' ti). The attainment of MOKSHA while living in the body. An individual who has attained jivanmukti lives in the consciousness of God.

jivatman (jī' vāt man). The ATMAN manifesting itself as the individual self.

jnana (gñā' na). 1. Knowledge. 2. Knowledge of the ultimate Reality; the transcendental realization that Atman and Brahman are one.

Jnanakanda (gñā' na kān' da). *See* VEDA.

jnana yoga (gñā' na yo' ga). The path of knowledge; one of the four main yogas, or paths to union with the Divine. By analyzing and then rejecting all transitory phenomena, through the process of elimination the spiritual aspirant finally comes to Brahman and realizes his union with the impersonal aspect of the Godhead.

jnani (gñā' nī). 1. One who follows the path of knowledge and discrimination to reach the impersonal Reality; a nondualist. 2. A knower of Brahman.

Jogin (jo' gīn). *See* Swami YOGANANDA.

Jogin Ma (jo' gīn mā'), also Yogin Ma. Jogindra Mohini Mitra, 1851-1924, a woman disciple of Sri Ramakrishna and close companion of Sri SARADA DEVI. *See also* PANCHATAPA.

Kabir (ka bīr'). An Indian mystic of the weaver caste, who lived in the latter part of the 15th and the early part of the 16th centuries. His hymns and sayings exercised great influence on Moslems as well as Hindus.

Kailas (kai' lās). A mountain in the Himalayas, both real and mythical. Regarded as the abode of Shiva, it is a famous place of pilgrimage.

kaivalya (kai' val ya). A term used in raja yoga, defined by Swami Vivekananda as follows: "When the soul realizes that it depends on nothing in the universe, from gods to the lowest atom, that is called *kaivalya* (isolation) and perfection. It is attained when . . . the mind has been made as pure as the PURUSHA itself . . ."

Kali (kā′ lī), also Kalika. 1. A name of the Divine Mother. Kali is usually pictured as dancing on the breast of the inert Shiva, her husband, who symbolizes the transcendent aspect of Spirit whereas she symbolizes the dynamic aspect, the Primal Energy. Wearing a girdle of severed arms and a necklace of skulls, Kali holds the bleeding head of a demon in her lower left hand, a sword in the upper left. She makes the sign of fearlessness with the upper right hand and offers boons with the lower right—destroying ignorance, preserving world order, and blessing and liberating those who yearn for God-realization. Kali is the deity of the well-known temple dedicated to her at Dakshineswar, and was worshiped there for many years by Sri Ramakrishna. *See also* SHAKTI.

Kali (kā′ lī). Pre-monastic name of Swami ABHEDANANDA.

Kalighat (kā′ lī ghāt′). The famous temple of Kali in southern Calcutta; also the section of the city in which this temple is located. (It was the mispronunciation of Kalighat by the English which gave the city of Calcutta its name.)

Kali yuga (ka′ li yu′ ga). The fourth world period, which is supposed to comprise 432,000 years, and through which the world is said to be passing at present. *See* YUGA.

Kalpataru (kal′ pa ta′ ru). Lit., "Wish-fulfilling Tree." 1. A name of God. 2. The celestial tree of Hindu mythology, which grants all that a person under it desires.

kama (kā′ ma). 1. Craving. 2. Legitimate desire, the fulfillment of which is one of the FOUR FRUITS of human life.

Kamarpukur (kā′ mār pu′ kur). The village in West Bengal, *ca.* 75 miles northwest of Calcutta, where Sri Ramakrishna was born.

Kapila (ka′ pi la). The founder of SANKHYA philosophy.

karika (kā' ri kā). Comment or gloss.

karma (kar' ma). A mental or physical act; the consequence of a mental or physical act; the sum of the consequences of an individual's actions in this and previous lives; the chain of cause and effect operating in the moral world. Each individual's karma is made up of his SAMSKARAS. These potentialities guide his motives and conduct in the present as well as his future thoughts and actions. Thus every karma becomes a seed of another karma. The fruits of karma are reaped in the form of happiness or misery, according to the nature of each thought or act. Although each person imposes upon himself the limitation of his own character as determined by his past thoughts and actions, at the same time he can choose to follow the tendency he has formed or to struggle against it. The area of choice or free will in each individual reflects the freedom of the Atman, the indwelling Spirit. Devotion to God, enhancing good karmas and mitigating evil ones, begins to loosen the bonds of karma. When a man achieves illumination, his acts cease to produce karmas. *See also* AGAMI KARMA; PRARABDHA KARMA; SANCHITA KARMA. In the Vedas, karma means also ritualistic worship and philanthropic deeds.

Karmakanda (kar' ma kān' da). *See* VEDA.

karma yoga (kar' ma yo' ga). One of the four main yogas, or paths to union with the Divine: the path of selfless work, in which the spiritual aspirant offers every action and its results to God as a sacrament. The spiritual aspirant may also practice the attitude of considering himself the witness of actions and not the doer, regarding himself as the ATMAN (separate from the GUNAS, which act and react).

Kartika (kār' ti ka). A Hindu deity, son of Shiva and Parvati, known as Subrahmanya in southern India.

Kashi (kā' shī). A name of VARANASI.

Kashipur (kā' shī pur), also spelled Cossipore. A northern suburb of Calcutta, where Sri Ramakrishna lived (from December, 1885, until his passing away in August, 1886) in a garden house at 90 Kashipur Road.

Kathamrita (ka tām′ ri ta). Bengali name of the Gospel of Sri Ramakrishna. *See also* GUPTA.

Kausalya (kau′ sal yā). The mother of Sri Rama.

kayastha (kā′ yas ta). *See* CASTE.

Kedarnath (ke′ dār nāt). 1. A name of Shiva. 2. One of the chief places of pilgrimage in India—a temple on a mountain top in the Himalayas, dedicated to the worship of Kedarnath. 3. A temple in Varanasi, also dedicated to the worship of Kedarnath.

Keshab (ke′ shab). *See* SEN.

Keshava (ke′ sha va). A name of Sri Krishna.

Khudiram (khu′ di rām). Khudiram Chattopadhyaya, 1775-1843, the father of Sri Ramakrishna.

kirtan (kīr′ tan). Devotional singing or chanting.

kosha (ko′ sha). Sheath, covering. Five koshas, described in the Taittiriya Upanishad, are located one within the other and envelop the ATMAN. Beginning with the outermost sheath, they are: 1. Annamaya-kosha, the gross physical sheath, which is nourished by food. 2. Pranamaya-kosha, the subtle or vital sheath, which vitalizes and holds together body and mind. As long as this vital principle exists in the organism, life continues. The gross manifestation of this sheath is breath. 3. Manomaya-kosha, the sheath of mind, which receives sense impressions. 4. Vijnanamaya-kosha, the sheath of intellect, referring to the faculty which discriminates or wills. 5. Anandamaya-kosha, the sheath of bliss (referring to the ego or causal body), so called because it is nearest the blissful Atman. The Atman remains separate from the sheaths and unaffected by their properties.

Krishna (krish′ na). One of the most widely worshiped

Incarnations of Hinduism, Sri Krishna appears prominently
in the Mahabharata and the Bhagavatam. Among the most
popular of his forms are those of Baby Krishna (Gopala); of
the young Krishna playing his flute (beloved friend of the
cowherd boys and milkmaids of Brindavan); and of the Divine
Teacher of the Bhagavad-Gita (friend and charioteer of Arjuna), who ultimately reveals himself as the Universal Being.

kriya yoga (kri′ yā yo′ ga). Preliminary disciplines of
RAJA YOGA, which consist of three steps: AUSTERITY; study (the
reading of holy books, also the practice of JAPA); and dedication of the fruits of one's work to God.

kshatriya (kshat′ ri ya). *See* CASTE.

kumbhaka (kum′ bha ka). 1. Retention of the breath, between exhalation (rechaka) and inhalation (puraka) or inhalation and exhalation; a process described in raja and hatha
yoga. 2. Suspension of the breath, an attainment resulting
either from PRANAYAMA or from a natural spiritual development. A concentrated mind is the effect of kumbhaka when
artificially induced by breathing exercises. Kumbhaka is the
effect of a concentrated mind when it arises as a result of
natural spiritual development. The safer method of attaining
kumbhaka is to let the mind become absorbed in its object of
concentration naturally, through devotion to God; breathing
in this case ceases spontaneously, without any damaging effect
on body or mind.

kundalini (kun′ da li nī). Lit., "coiled up," like a serpent;
the spiritual energy lying dormant in human beings at the base
of the spine. When this energy awakens in a spiritual aspirant
and passes through the CENTERS OF CONSCIOUSNESS in the central spinal canal, it manifests itself in mystic experiences and
various degrees of illumination.

Kurukshetra (ku′ ruk she tra). The battlefield—situated
a few miles from the site of what is now New Delhi—where

the war between the Pandavas and Kauravas was fought, and where—as described in the BHAGAVAD-GITA—Sri Krishna taught Arjuna divine knowledge. Kurukshetra has been symbolically interpreted as the battlefield of life, representing the individual's struggle against his lower nature. *See also* MAHA-BHARATA.

kusha grass (ku′ sha). A type of grass (*Eragrostis cynosuroides*), used in some Hindu ritual worships.

kuthi (ku′ ti). 1. House, hut, cottage. 2. (*cap.*) Specif., the two-storied house in the Dakshineswar temple compound, which served as a residence of Rani RASMANI and her family. Sri Ramakrishna also spent much time there during the Rani's and MATHUR's lifetime.

Lakshmana (laksh′ ma na). A brother of Sri Rama.

Lakshmi (laksh′ mī). The Divine Mother as Goddess of Wealth and consort of Vishnu.

Latu (lā′ tu). *See* Swami ADBHUTANANDA.

liberation. Same as MOKSHA.

lila (lī′ lā). The divine play, in which the same actor—God—enacts all the roles, so to speak. The whole universe is said to be created by him as sport, for his pleasure. A special manifestation of lila is the AVATAR. Lila, moreover, means the Relative (which consists of time, space, and causation).

Lilaprasanga (lī′ lā pra sang′ ga). The *Sri Sri Ramakrishna Lilaprasanga*, by Swami SARADANANDA, which was translated as *Sri Ramakrishna the Great Master*.

linga (ling′ ga), also lingam. Lit., "symbol" or "sign"; a representation of SHIVA. The linga is shaped like a pillar and rounded at the top; at its foot a surrounding basin catches the offerings. It is the emblem generally used in the ritual worship of Shiva, and it represents a transition from the anthropomorphic to the formless conception of the deity. Lingas are often made of stone. They vary in size and somewhat in shape;

some are natural formations, some man-made. Swami Vivekananda traces the origin of the linga to the hymn in the
Atharva Veda Samhita sung in praise of Yupa-Stambha, the
sacrificial post.

loka (lo' ka). Sphere or plane of existence.

lotus. A metaphor frequently used in Indian literature. 1.
A figurative description of the CENTERS OF CONSCIOUSNESS in
the human body. The "lotus of the heart" (anahata) and the
"thousand-petaled lotus" in the brain (sahasrara) are frequently indicated to the spiritual aspirant as places in which
to concentrate the mind on the Chosen Ideal of God. 2. Deities are often described as having lotus-eyes or lotus-feet—the
lotus representing beauty and holiness. 3. The lotus leaf,
which, though it rests on water, does not become wet, symbolizes NONATTACHMENT.

luchi (lu' chi). A rich Indian bread, made from white
flour and fried in butter.

M. *See* GUPTA.

Madhava (mä' dha va). Lit., "the Sweet One"; a name of
Sri Krishna.

madhura (ma dhu' ra). *See* BHAKTI YOGA.

Madhva (madh' va), 1199-1276, an exponent of the dualistic school of VEDANTA and celebrated commentator on the Vedanta Sutras, the Gita, and the Upanishads. According to
Madhva's philosophy, matter, God, and human souls are absolutely different from one another. God is the ruler of the universe, the universe being real and eternally existent.

Mahabharata (ma hä' bhä' ra ta). Perhaps the world's
longest epic poem, consisting of some 110,000 couplets—in-
cluding the BHAGAVAD-GITA. This famous Hindu epic, known
as a treasure house of Indian lore, is divided into 18 books
called parvas. Its earliest composition has been estimated at
not later than the 5th century B.C. Expanding upon and illus-

trating the truths of the Vedas, the Mahabharata tells the story of King Bharata's descendants—the PANDAVAS and Kauravas, who were cousins. According to Vyasa, the reputed author of the epic, the purpose of the Mahabharata is to sing the glory of God—the dynastic war between the Pandavas and Kauravas merely providing the occasion.

mahabhava (ma hā′ bhā′ va). *See* BHAKTI YOGA.

Mahadeva (ma hā′ de′ va). Lit., "the Great God"; a name of Shiva.

Mahamaya (ma hā′ mā′ yā). The Mother of the Universe. On the one hand, her divine play veils man's vision of Brahman, making the one Reality appear as the manifold universe. On the other hand, through her grace ignorance vanishes, and man realizes his identity with Brahman.

Maharaj (ma′ hā rāj). Lit., "great king"; lord, master. 1. A title of respect used to address Indian holy men—either instead of the name or following the first name (*e.g.*, Abani Maharaj). 2. In the Ramakrishna Order, a term often specifically applied to Swami BRAHMANANDA.

mahasamadhi (ma hā′ sa mā′ dhi). Lit., "the great samadhi," or superconscious state. The word almost always refers to the final absorption in the Divine of an illumined soul when the body is given up.

mahat (ma′ hat). Cosmic intelligence. *See* COSMIC EVOLUTION.

mahavakya (ma hā′ vāk′ ya). Lit., "great saying"; a terse Vedantic formula, or mantra, stating the oneness of the individual soul with BRAHMAN. There is a mahavakya in each of the four Vedas: 1. "Consciousness is Brahman" ("Prajnanam Brahma"), in the Aitareya Upanishad of the Rig-Veda; 2. "I am Brahman" ("Aham Brahmasmi"), in the Brihadaranyaka Upanishad of the Yajur Veda; 3. "That thou art" ("Tat tvam asi"), in the Chandogya Upanishad of the Sama Veda; 4.

"This Self is Brahman" ("Ayam Atma Brahma"), in the Mandukya Upanishad of the Atharva Veda.

Mahavir (ma' hā vīr'), or Mahavira. Lit., "great hero"; a name of HANUMAN.

Maheshvara (ma hesh' va ra). Lit., "great Lord"; a name of Shiva.

manas (ma' nas). A component of the mind which receives sense impressions from the outside world and presents them to the BUDDHI. Manas, moreover, carries out the orders of the will through the organs of action. *See also* COSMIC EVOLUTION.

manipura chakra (ma' ni pū ra   chak' ra). The third of seven yogic CENTERS OF CONSCIOUSNESS in the human body, located near the navel.

manomaya-kosha (ma no' ma ya ko' sha). The sheath of mind. *See* KOSHA.

mantra (man' tra), also mantram. 1. The particular name of God, corresponding to the CHOSEN IDEAL of the disciple, with which the latter is initiated into spiritual life by his GURU. The mantra, regarded as one with God, represents the essence of the guru's instruction to his disciple, who is enjoined to keep it sacred and secret, and to meditate on the aspect of God which it symbolizes for the rest of his life. Repetition of the mantra (JAPA), performed regularly and reverently, results in purification of the mind, and ultimately in God-realization. *See also* BIJA MANTRA; INITIATION; PURASCHARANA. 2. Sacred word, verse, or Vedic hymn.

Manu (ma' nu). The ancient lawgiver, whose code is the foundation of Hindu religious and social conduct.

Master. *See* THAKUR.

math (mat). A monastery.

Mathur (ma' tur). Mathuranath Bishwas, son-in-law of Rani RASMANI. Mathur was deeply devoted to Sri Ramakrishna, providing him with all material necessities for 14 years at

Dakshineswar. He died in 1871.

Mathura (ma′ tu rā). A city in Uttar Pradesh, India, believed to have been Sri Krishna's birthplace, and the capital where he ruled as king.

maya (mā′ yā). A universal principle of Vedanta philosophy, which is the basis of mind and matter. Maya is BRAH-MAN's power; in this sense, maya is eternally inseparable from Brahman, related to him as the heat of fire is related to fire. United, maya and Brahman constitute Ishvara (the Personal God), who creates, preserves, and dissolves the universe. In another sense, as Ignorance, or Cosmic Illusion, maya is a superimposition upon Brahman. Maya veils man's vision of Brahman, as a result of which man perceives the manifold universe instead of the one Reality. Maya has two aspects: avidya (ignorance) and vidya (knowledge). Avidya-maya, leading man farther away from the realization of Brahman into greater worldliness and bondage, expresses itself in passions and cravings. (Ignorance is beginningless, but it has an end for each individual when he attains spiritual illumination.) Vidya-maya, leading man closer to realization of Brahman, expresses itself in spiritual virtues. Vidya and avidya are aspects of the Relative (within time, space, and causation); man transcends vidya and avidya when he realizes Brahman, the Absolute.

meditation. Technically speaking, the state of DHYANA— prolonged concentration, achieved through repeated practice. As generally used by Vedanta devotees, the word denotes efforts to achieve PRATYAHARA and DHARANA. Both meanings differ from the Christian concept of meditation as a more or less discursive operation of the mind around a central spiritual idea or scene.

Mimamsa. Same as PURVA MIMAMSA.

Mirabai (mī′ rā bā′ i), 1547-1614, queen of Chitore and

mystic poetess, renowned for her devotion to Sri Krishna. She
renounced the world and lived a dedicated life at Brindavan.

moksha (mok' sha). Final liberation from karma and reincarnation—*i.e.*, from all worldly bondage—through union
with God or knowledge of the ultimate Reality. Moksha is the
highest of the FOUR FRUITS or goals of human life.

mridanga (mri dang' ga). A barrel-shaped Indian drum,
about two feet long, with a head on each end, both played
simultaneously.

mudra (mud' rā). A symbolic hand gesture. The mudras
in the Hindu ritual worship (or PUJA), designed to connect
external actions with spiritual ideas, serve as aids in concentrating the mind on God.

mukti (muk' ti). Same as MOKSHA.

muladhara chakra (mū' lā dhā' ra   chak' ra). The first
and lowest of seven yogic CENTERS OF CONSCIOUSNESS in the
human body, located at the base of the spine.

mysticism. The belief that direct knowledge of God can be
attained, as it has been attained by the saints and mystics of
all religions. The culmination of mystic experience (NIRVANA,
or SAMADHI), is reached in the superconscious state. Hindus
and Buddhists believe that this state can be experienced on
earth while living in a human body.

Nada-Brahman (nā' da bra' man).   Lit., "sound-Brah-
man"; same as OM.

Nag, Durga Charan (nāg,   dur' gā   cha' ran). Popularly
known as Nag Mahashay, 1846-1899, he was a householder-
disciple of Sri Ramakrishna, endowed with exemplary humility, renunciation, and devotion to God and to his guru.

nahabat (na' ha bat). A music tower or bandstand. There
are two nahabats at the Dakshineswar temple garden, one of
which was occupied by Sri Ramakrishna's mother and wife.

nama (nā' ma), or nam. Name; name of God.

namah (na′ ma). Salutation; used in a prayer or MANTRA. In some combinations, namah becomes "namo"—as for instance in "Namo Narayanaya." This sacred mantra (a salutation to one of Vishnu's forms) also serves as a greeting between monks.

namaskar (na′ mas kār). Lit., "act of salutation"; a popular greeting among persons of more or less equal rank. *See also* PRANAM.

namaste (na′ mas te). Lit., "Salutation to you"; a popular greeting throughout India.

namo. *See* NAMAH.

Nanak (nā′ nak), often called Guru Nanak, 1469-1538. The founder of Sikhism, and the first of the ten Gurus of this Indian religion. His gospel—God's unity, man's brotherhood, faith, and love—attracted Hindus and Moslems alike.

Nandi (nan′ di). One of Shiva's chief devotees, and his mount, having the form of a bull. Nandi is said to have assumed this animal body because the human frame was not strong enough to contain his ecstatic devotion.

Nangta (nāng′ tā). Lit., "the Naked One"; the name by which Sri Ramakrishna referred to TOTA PURI.

Narada (nā′ ra da). A great Hindu saint, mentioned in the Rig-Veda and in the Puranas.

Narada Bhakti Sutras (nā′ ra da bhak′ ti sū′ tras). NARADA's aphorisms on bhakti (divine love).

Narayana (nā′ rā′ ya na). Lit., "Mover on the waters"; a name of Vishnu.

Narayani (nā′ rā′ ya nī). The consort of NARAYANA; a name of the Divine Mother.

Narendranath (na ren′ dra nāt′), also Naren, Narendra. Boyhood names of Swami VIVEKANANDA.

Narmada (nar′ ma dā). A sacred river of India.

Nataraja (na′ ta rā′ ja). SHIVA as king of dancers, or lord of the stage of this world. His dance represents his five activities: creation, preservation, destruction, embodiment, and liberation. One foot crushes the demon Muyalaka (symbol of ignorance and worldliness), the other foot, raised upward, represents the superconscious state. The place of the dance is the body (of the individual as well as of the cosmos). The circle of flames within which he dances has been interpreted as the dance of nature compared with Shiva's dance of wisdom; his dance has also been identified with the syllable OM, the fiery arch being the hook of the ideograph of the written sign. Coomaraswamy's *The Dance of Shiva* deals in detail with the profuse symbolism inspired by this form.

natmandir (nāt' man' dir). A hall, built in front of a temple for the performance of religious plays, music, and discourses.

Navadvip (na' vad vīp). A town in Bengal where Sri CHAITANYA was born.

New Dispensation. A sect of the BRAHMO SAMAJ, headed by Keshab Chandra SEN.

Nimbarka (nim bār' ka). A saintly Hindu philosopher, who taught the doctrine of Bhedabheda (duality in nonduality). According to Nimbarka, Brahman is both personal and impersonal; and the individual soul is part of Brahman as well as one with him. Nimbarka laid stress upon both knowledge and devotion as means to the attainment of liberation.

Niranjan. *See* Swami NIRANJANANANDA.

Niranjanananda, Swami (ni ran' ja nā' nan da). Nityaniranjan Ghosh, *ca.* 1863-1904, a monastic disciple of Sri Ramakrishna. Niranjan came to Dakshineswar between 1881 and 1882. He served Sri Ramakrishna at Kashipur, and after the latter's passing away joined his brother monks at Baranagore and afterwards at Alambazar. He accompanied Swami Vivekananda on a tour of northern India, and later spent some

time in Varanasi. Swami Niranjanananda was one of six disciples whom Sri Ramakrishna regarded as belonging to the
class of ISHVARAKOTIS.

nirbija samadhi (nir bī′ ja   sa mā′ dhi). Lit., "seedless
samadhi"; a term of Yoga philosophy referring to the supreme
superconscious state, in which all thought-waves are completely stilled and all sense of duality is obliterated. *See also* NIR-
VANA.

Nirguna Brahman (nir′ gu na   bra′ man). The unconditioned Absolute; Brahman without attributes.

nirvana (nir vā′ na). State of spiritual enlightenment or
illumination, characterized by extinction or absorption of the
individual and ephemeral ego in BRAHMAN (which the Buddhists call the "Uncaused" and "Unconditioned"). Nirvana releases man from the cycle of birth, suffering, death, and all
other forms of worldly bondage. It is the supreme transcendental consciousness—called Brahma-nirvana in the Gita, TURIYA
in the Upanishads, nirvana in Buddhism, nirbija samadhi in
Yoga, and nirvikalpa samadhi in Vedanta.

nirvichara samadhi (nir′ vi chā′ ra   sa mā′ dhi). A term
of Yoga philosophy, referring to the state of absorption in
which the mind achieves identity with a subtle object of concentration, unmixed with awareness of name, quality, and
knowledge. *See also* NIRVANA.

nirvikalpa samadhi (nir′ vi kal′ pa   sa mā′ dhi). Lit.,
"changeless samadhi"; a term of Vedanta philosophy referring
to the supreme transcendental state of consciousness, in which
the spiritual aspirant becomes completely absorbed in Brahman so that all sense of duality is obliterated. *See also* NIR-
VANA.

Nitya (nit′ ya). The ultimate Reality; the eternal Absolute.

Nityananda (nit′ yā nan da), also Nitai. An intimate disciple of Sri Chaitanya.

nityasiddha (nit' ya sid' dha). Lit., "eternally perfect"; same as ISHVARAKOTI.

niyama (ni' ya ma). Observance of certain virtues; the second of the eight limbs of raja yoga. The virtues are purity (physical and mental); contentment; AUSTERITY, which may include the performance of worship (PUJA); study (the reading of holy books as well as practice of JAPA); and devotion to God.

nonattachment. Patanjali defines nonattachment as "self-mastery," "freedom from desire for what is seen or heard." Attached to God alone, the nonattached individual does not crave possession of sense objects and attractions or of the fruits of his actions. He performs his work as KARMA YOGA and considers the world and all living beings as manifestations of the Divine. Nonattachment therefore does not mean indifference to one's work and fellow men; on the contrary, it denotes a profound regard for them—but without the sense of "me" and "mine."

nondualism. *See* VEDANTA; VEDANTA SCHOOLS OF THOUGHT.

nyasa (nyā' sa). Mental assignation of various parts of the body to presiding deities during the Hindu ritual worship, or PUJA, accompanied by prayers and gestures.

Nyaya (nyā' ya). School of Indian logic, systematized by Gotama; one of the six DARSHANAS (systems of Hindu thought).

occult power. Psychic power or control (siddhi, in Sanskrit), which may arise through the practice of concentration of mind. Occult powers include the ability to make oneself invisible, to fly through the air, to read others' minds, etc. These powers obstruct spiritual progress and must be renounced if the aspirant wishes to advance toward God-realization.

ojas (o' jas). Lit., "the illuminating" or "bright"; the highest form of energy in the human body. In the spiritual aspirant who constantly practices continence and purity, other forms of energy are transmuted into ojas and stored in the brain, expressing as spiritual and intellectual power.

Om (om), sometimes spelled Aum. The sacred syllable representing the impersonal Absolute as well as the personal aspect of God; the Logos. Om is the undifferentiated Word which has produced all manifestation. Swami Vivekananda says about this most basic and comprehensive of all sounds: "The first letter, *A,* is the root sound, the key, pronounced without touching any part of the tongue or palate; *M* represents the last sound in the series, being produced by the closed lips, and the *U* rolls from the very root to the end of the sounding-board of the mouth. Thus, Om represents the whole phenomenon of sound-producing." Repetition of Om with meditation on its meaning is prescribed as an effective spiritual practice.

Om Tat Sat (om tat sat). Lit., "Om That is Being"; sacred words used to invoke the Divine.

Panchadashi (pan' cha da shī'). A 14th-century treatise on nondualistic Vedanta.

panchatapa (pan' cha ta' pa). A severe austerity, which is observed by sitting for JAPA and meditation from dawn till sunset, encircled by four fires, with the sun blazing overhead. Sri SARADA DEVI and JOGIN MA once practiced this spiritual discipline for a week.

Panchavati (pan' cha va' ti). A grove of five sacred trees, designed as a place in which to practice spiritual disciplines. The trees which must be used are: an ASHVATTHA, a BANYAN, a BEL, an AMALAKI, and an ASHOKA. They are planted in a circle, according to scriptural injunctions, and an altar is placed in the center. The Panchavati at the Dakshineswar temple garden was planted by Sri Ramakrishna and HRIDAY.

Pandava (pān' da va). Any one of the five sons of King Pandu: Yudhishthira, Bhima, Arjuna, Nakula, and Sahadeva.

Their lives are described in the MAHABHARATA.

pandit (pan' dit), also pundit. A scholar, learned in the scriptures.

para-bhakti (pa rā' bhak' ti). Supreme devotion to God.

Parabrahman (pa' ra bra' man). The supreme BRAHMAN.

paramahamsa (pa' ra ma ham' sa). 1. A monk who belongs to the highest order of knowers of Brahman; *(cap.)* a term often applied to Sri Ramakrishna. 2. A monk who belongs to a particular sect of the Shankara Order.

Paramatman (pa' ra māt' man). The supreme ATMAN.

para-vidya (pa' rā vid' yā). Supreme knowledge; *i.e.*, the transcendental knowledge of Brahman.

Parvati (pār' va tī), or Uma. One of the many forms of the Divine Mother. Parvati is the daughter of King Himalaya and the consort of Shiva.

Patanjali (pa tan' ja li). The compiler of the YOGA SUTRAS.

Pavhari Baba (pav' hā ri bā' bā). A Hindu saint of the 19th century, much revered by Swami Vivekananda.

payas (pā' yas). A sweet milk pudding.

pingala (ping' ga lā). A column of sensory and motor fibers on the right side of the spinal cord. *See* SUSHUMNA.

Prahlada (pra lā' da). Son of the demon king Hiranyakashipu, mentioned in the Bhagavatam, who remained steadfast in devotion to Vishnu, his Chosen Ideal, despite repeated torture and attempts on his life devised by his evil father.

Prajapati (pra jā' pa ti). A name of Brahma, God as Creator.

prakriti (pra' kri ti). One of two ultimate realities postulated by SANKHYA philosophy. Prakriti denotes primordial nature; it is composed of three GUNAS and constitutes the material of the universe. By its proximity to PURUSHA, prakriti evolves as the world of mind and matter. *See also* COSMIC EVOLUTION.

prana (prā' na). The sum total of primal energy, from

which all mental and physical energy has evolved. Prana manifests, for instance, as motion, gravitation, magnetism, the vital principle which sustains physical life, thought force, and bodily action. Five modifications of prana (prana, apana, vyana, udana, and samana) are concerned with such bodily functions as breathing, digesting, eliminating, assimilating food, etc.

prana (prā′ nā). Lit., "whose life is in . . ."—a designation forming the last part of names of PRAVRAJIKAS affiliated with the Ramakrishna Order, or, in India, with the Sarada Math; *e.g.,* Yogaprana ("whose life is in yoga").

pranam (pra nām′). Respectful salutation to the Lord or to a superior or elder—with folded palms, or by taking the dust of the feet (touching the superior's feet and then one's own forehead with the right hand or with both hands), or by prostrating.

pranamaya-kosha (prā′ na ma ya ko′ sha). The vital sheath. *See* KOSHA.

pranayama (prā′ nā yā′ ma). Control of the vital energy (PRANA) through the practice of breathing exercises; the fourth of the eight limbs of raja yoga. Unless rules of strict continence and diet are observed and supervision by a competent teacher is obtained, the practice of pranayama may produce mental and physical disorders. *See also* KUMBHAKA.

prarabdha karma (prā′ rab dha kar′ ma). That portion of stored-up KARMA from past lives which has begun to bear fruit in the present life, in which it must be exhausted.

prasad (pra sād′). Food or any other gift which has been ceremonially offered to God or to a saintly person; it is usually afterwards given to devotees. A recipient of prasad considers himself blessed and purified.

pratyahara (prat′ yā hā′ ra). Withdrawal of the mind from sense-objects; the fifth of the eight limbs of raja yoga.

Pravrajika (pra vrā′ ji kā). The title of SANNYASINIS affiliated with the Ramakrishna Order, or, in India, with the Sarada Math (corresponding to the title of Swami for sannyasins). The generic meaning of the word is "woman ascetic."

prema (pre′ ma). Ecstatic love of God. *See* BHAKTI YOGA.

Premananda, Swami (pre′ mā′ nan da). Baburam Ghosh,
1861-1918, a monastic disciple of Sri Ramakrishna. Baburam,
whose sister was married to Balaram BOSE, came to Dakshineswar in 1882. Sri Ramakrishna, who regarded Baburam as one
belonging to the class of ISHVARAKOTIs, said that he was pure
to his very marrow. After Sri Ramakrishna's passing away,
Baburam joined his brother-disciples at Baranagore and afterwards at Alambazar. Later, he became head of the Belur
Math and vice-president of the Ramakrishna Order.

puja (pū′ jā). Hindu ritual worship. Puja is designed to
concentrate the mind on God and thus to heighten devotion.
It is offered to any one of the many aspects of the Supreme
Being—often to one of his divine forms (*e.g.,* Kali, Shiva; or
to an incarnation, such as Rama or Krishna). The deity may
be represented by an image, photograph, or other symbol.
Worship may be performed with sandalpaste and flowers; or
with five items (sandalpaste, flower, incense stick, light, and
food); or with ten items (water for washing feet, ARGHYA, water
for sipping, for bathing, for rinsing mouth and hands, in addition to the five items mentioned above). In most centers of
the Ramakrishna Order a ten-item worship to the Lord is performed daily for the benefit of the whole religious community,
and the food offering is distributed afterwards as PRASAD. A
sixteen-item worship is performed on special days, such as
Kali puja, the birthday of Sri Ramakrishna, etc. In some Ramakrishna monasteries, Jesus is honored with a Hindu ritual
worship at Christmastime. Each gesture or action during a
puja must be done with the worshiper's mind concentrated on
its symbolic significance, which serves to remind him that de-

ity, offerings, utensils, and devotee are BRAHMAN. The ritual worship is therefore basically nondualistic. The meditations accompanying it embrace Vedanta philosophy, metaphysics, and mythology, and are concretized in the accessories used. Puja reconciles the path of devotion with the path of knowledge, ranging, as it does, from the devotee's meditation on his identity with Brahman to worship of the deity as an honored guest, physically present.

pujari (pū' jā' rī). A male person who performs ritualistic worship. Feminine: pujarini.

Purana (pu rā' na). Lit., "ancient"; any one of eighteen sacred books of Hinduism, attributed to VYASA, which elaborate and popularize the spiritual truths of the Vedas by means of illustrations from the lives of divine incarnations, saints, kings, and devotees, whether historical or mythological.

purascharana (pu ras' cha ra na). The performance of JAPA a certain number of times each day, methodically increasing and decreasing the amount. The aspirant may begin on the first day after the new moon by repeating his MANTRA one thousand times, increasing the amount by a thousand each day until he reaches fifteen thousand on the day of the full moon. Then he decreases his japa by a thousand each day, coming down to one thousand at the next new moon. Such a practice may be continued over a period of one or more years, as the guru directs.

Puri (pu' ri). Seashore town in the state of Orissa; one of the principal holy places of India. *See also* JAGANNATH.

Puri (pu' rī). One of the ten denominations of the Shankara Order, to which the Ramakrishna Order belongs.

puri (pū' rī). A type of Indian bread, made from wholewheat flour and fried in deep fat.

Purna (pūr' na). Purna Chandra Ghosh, a householder-disciple of Sri Ramakrishna, born *ca.* 1872, who came to Dak-

shineswar about 1885. Sri Ramakrishna regarded him as an
ISHVARAKOTI.

Purusha (pu′ ru sha). One of the two ultimate realities
postulated by SANKHYA philosophy, Purusha denotes the Self,
the Absolute, Spirit, Pure Consciousness. Purusha is the witness of the changes of PRAKRITI. *See also* COSMIC EVOLUTION.
In Vedanta philosophy, Purusha denotes the ATMAN.

Purva Mimamsa (pūr′ va mī mām′ sā). One of the six
DARSHANAS (systems of orthodox Hindu philosophy), whose
chief exponent was Jaimini. Purva Mimamsa is closely related
to Hindu law. Its main objectives are to establish the authority
of the Vedas as the supreme source of all knowledge, to eluci-
date the meaning of their ritual portions, and to emphasize
the importance of performing their ceremonies.

qualified nondualism. *See* VISHISHTADVAITA.

Radha (rā′ dhā), also Radhika. Chief GOPI of Brindavan.

Radhakanta (rā′ dhā kān′ ta). Lit., "beloved of Radha";
a name of Sri Krishna. The image of the deity consists of two
figures, Radha and Krishna. At the Radhakanta temple in the
Dakshineswar temple garden, Sri Ramakrishna and his
brother Ramkumar both served as priests. When the image of
the deity was damaged in an accident, Sri Ramakrishna per-
sonally repaired it.

Radhu (rā′ dhu). A niece of Sri SARADA DEVI. Responsibility for Radhu served as a weight—a mundane adjunct—for
the Holy Mother's mind, keeping it, for the purpose of teaching mankind, from its natural tendency to be completely
merged in samadhi.

raga (rā′ ga). Melody type; the basis of Indian musical
composition.

raga bhakti (rā′ ga bhak′ ti). Spontaneous divine love,
stemming from intense attachment to God.

Raghuvir (ra′ ghu vīr). Lit., "hero of the Raghus"; a name of Sri Rama. Raghuvir was the family deity of Sri Rama-krishna.

rajas (ra' jas). *See* GUNA.

rajasic (rā' ja sik). Pertaining to or characterized by the GUNA of rajas.

raja yoga (rā' ja yo' ga). Lit., "royal yoga"; one of the four main yogas, or paths to union with the Divine, systematized in the YOGA SUTRAS of Patanjali. Raja yoga is the path of formal meditation, a method of concentrating the mind one-pointedly on the ultimate Reality until complete absorption is achieved. The eight limbs of raja yoga are 1. YAMA; 2. NIYAMA; 3. ASANA; 4. PRANAYAMA; 5. PRATYAHARA; 6. DHARANA; 7. DHYANA; 8. SAMADHI (absorption). *See also* KAIVALYA; KRIYA YOGA; SAMYAMA.

Rakhal (rā' khāl). Boyhood name of Swami BRAHMA-NANDA.

Ram (rām). *See* DATTA.

Rama (rā' ma), also Ramachandra. One of the most popular divine incarnations of Hinduism, king of Ayodhya, and hero of the RAMAYANA.

Ramakrishna (rā' ma krish' na), 1836-1886, a God-man of unique spiritual capacity, whose life inspired the modern renaissance of Vedanta. After realizing his union with God through various paths within Hinduism, as well as through Christianity and Islam, Sri Ramakrishna proclaimed that the ultimate Reality can be known by a follower of any religion if his devotion is equal to the task. Sri Ramakrishna was born in KAMARPUKUR as Gadadhar Chattopadhyaya. His UPANA-YANA ceremony took place in 1845. In 1852, he joined his brother Ramkumar in Calcutta, and in 1855, at the DAKSHINES-WAR temple garden. Between 1855 and 1864, he practiced intensively a variety of spiritual disciplines. In 1856, he became priest of the Kali temple, and at this time had his first vision of the Divine Mother. In 1859, Sri Ramakrishna was betrothed to Saradamani (*see* SARADA DEVI). In 1861, the BHAIRAVI BRAHMANI and two well-known pandits proclaimed him to be an AVATAR. Between 1862 and 63, he underwent Tantric disciplines under the Bhairavi Brahmani. In 1864, he practiced one after another the vatsalya and madhura attitudes of BHAKTI YOGA, worshiping RAMLALA and Sri Krishna until he saw them in vision; he was initiated into sannyas and nondual Vedanta by Tota Puri, and reached NIRVIKALPA SAMADHI. In 1866, Sri Ramakrishna lived in the nirvikalpa state for about six months; later was initiated into Islam by the Sufi Govinda Rai. In 1868, he made a pilgrimage to VARANASI and BRINDAVAN. In 1870, he visited NAVADVIP. In 1872, his wife came to Dakshineswar for her first visit; and the same year Sri Ramakrishna performed the Shodashi puja, worshiping Sri Sarada Devi as the Divine Mother. His worship of Christ, in 1874, culminated in a vision of Jesus. In 1875, Sri Ramakrishna's association with Keshab SEN began; and in 1879, Ram Chandra Datta and Manomohan Mitra (his first householder-disciples) came to Dakshineswar. Between 1880 and 1885, Sri Ramakrishna's chief disciples and devotees gathered around him. Between 1882-85, the photo in which he is shown seated in samadhi, was taken. In 1885, the first symptoms of his throat cancer appeared; Sri Ramakrishna left Dakshineswar to stay with Balaram BOSE in Calcutta; then moved briefly to SHYAMPUKUR, and subsequently to KASHIPUR. On January 1, 1886, at Kashipur, Sri Ramakrishna's spiritual power manifested itself in a special way when he blessed many devotees and granted them God-realization. It was at Kashipur that the young disciples of his inner circle gathered to serve him and were trained by him, and thus the foundation of the future RAMAKRISHNA MATH AND MISSION was laid. Even during his lifetime, Sri Ramakrishna was accorded divine worship.

Since his passing away he has received widespread recognition as an incarnation of God. An introduction to his life and teachings is to be found in The Gospel of Sri Ramakrishna, compiled by M.

Ramakrishna Math and Mission (rā′ ma krish′ na mat′). A twin institution established in the name of Sri RAMAKRISHNA. The nucleus of the Math (lit., "monastery") was formed in 1886. Early that year, Sri Ramakrishna gave GERUA cloths and rosaries to 11 intimate disciples. In December 1886, at Antpur, nine of these pledged themselves to a life of renunciation; and in January 1887, before a homa fire, formal vows of sannyas were taken. Under the leadership of Swami VIVEKANANDA, the Math was organized for the purpose of training monks for the realization of God and for the service of humanity. After temporary quarters at BARANAGORE and ALAMBAZAR, the Math was transferred (in 1899) to its present headquarters at BELUR. The Mission was started in 1897, also under Swami Vivekananda's guidance, to promote social service and education as a joint effort of monastics and lay devotees. In India, the Mission has its own hospitals, dispensaries, high schools, industrial and agricultural schools, libraries, and publishing houses. In 1941, it opened a college (scheduled to be accredited as a university in 1963). The Mission has been consistently active in relieving victims of earthquakes, floods, famines, and epidemics. The Ramakrishna Math and Mission has inspired *ca.* 200 centers or groups—most of them in India, 25 or so in other parts of the world. To carry on the work of the first American Vedanta groups, inspired by Swami Vivekananda, four other direct disciples of Sri Ramakrishna came to the United States: Swamis SARADANANDA, ABHEDANANDA, TURIYANANDA, and TRIGUNATITA. From that time onward, the Ramakrishna Math has met an increasing demand for resident teachers. Each one of them has come to the United

States upon invitation of some group of Americans who wished to learn more about VEDANTA philosophy and practice. The Swamis are guest-teachers, not missionaries; and they work to help individuals deepen and progress in the religious tendencies of the devotees' own choice. There are now approximately a dozen Vedanta Societies in the United States. Although they are under the spiritual guidance of the Math, they are self-supporting, independent units, run by their own boards of trustees. Tied to Math and Mission through the resident Swami, their purpose is promotion of the study of Vedanta, as well as promotion of harmony between Eastern and Western thought, and recognition of the truth in all the great religions of the world. These purposes are pursued primarily by means of public lectures and study classes, and through personal instruction in prayer and meditation. Individuals who wish to associate themselves more closely with the work and are seriously interested in the teachings of Vedanta may apply for membership. This is open to all, regardless of creed or religious affiliation. Some of the American centers have monasteries and convents attached to them, where under the supervision of a Swami, monastic aspirants are trained in worship, meditation, and service, and have the opportunity to prepare themselves for BRAHMACHARYA and SANNYAS. (The *History of the Ramakrishna Math and Mission,* by Swami Gambhirananda, deals in detail with the development of the Ramakrishna movement and its institutions.)

Ramakrishnananda, Swami   (rā′ ma krish nā′ nan da). Shashibhushan Chakravarti, 1863-1911, a monastic disciple of Sri Ramakrishna. Shashi was the cousin of Sharat (*see* SARADANANDA). Sri Ramakrishna, whom the two boys first visited in 1883, regarded them as having been followers of Christ in a previous incarnation. Shashi served Sri Ramakrishna at Kashipur. After his guru's passing away he joined his monastic brothers at Baranagore, where he instituted the ritual worship of Sri Ramakrishna. In 1897, he went to Madras and established a Ramakrishna Mission center there. His extensive lecture tours of South India were instrumental in starting other centers also. Ramakrishnananda was an outstanding example of the spirit of service and of devotion to the guru.

Ramanuja (rā' mā' nu ja). A celebrated philosopher-saint of South India, 1017-1137, the founder of VISHISHTADVAITA. After renouncing the world, Ramanuja went to Srirangam where he wrote a commentary on the Vedanta Sutras, as he had promised before the corpse of his great-grandfather YA-MUNA that he would do. He also wrote commentaries on the Gita and some original philosophical treatises propounding his doctrine. According to Ramanuja, the highest ideal of human life is to love God and to live in self-surrender to him.

Ramayana (rā' mā' ya na). The most ancient Sanskrit epic poem, written by the sage Valmiki. It is estimated to have been composed about 500 B.C., and contains approximately 50,000 lines. The Ramayana describes the life of Sri RAMA: his banishment from AYODHYA; life in the forest with his faithful wife, SITA; Sita's abduction by RAVANA; the war of Rama and his allies against Ravana; defeat of Ravana and rescue of Sita; Rama's return to Ayodhya as ruler; slander of Sita by the people of Ayodhya and her banishment from the kingdom; her subsequent exoneration and final ascent to heaven, where she is joined by Rama.

Rameswar (rā' mesh war). Rameswar Chattopadhyaya, born 1826, older brother of Sri Ramakrishna.

Rameswaram (rā' mesh wa ram). A town in southern Madras State, one of the principal holy places of India. The deity in its most famous temple (Shiva) is said to have been installed by RAMA and SITA.

Ramkumar (rām' ku mār'), Ramkumar Chattopadhyaya,

1805-1856, oldest brother of Sri Ramakrishna.

Ramlal (rām' lāl). A nephew of Sri Ramakrishna.

Ramlala (rām' lā lā). The Boy RAMA. The living deity manifested itself through a metal image of Ramlala which was worshiped by Jatadhari, a wandering monk, and presented by him to Sri Ramakrishna about 1864.

Ram Nam (rām' nām'). A song service of ancient Hindu prayers, invoking the divine presence of RAMA, SITA, and HANUMAN. Popular in southern India, Ram Nam was introduced by Swami Brahmananda in centers of the Ramakrishna Order, to be sung on EKADASHI. It is performed with local variations in the ashramas where this tradition is observed.

Ramprasad (rām' pra sād'). A poet of Bengal, who lived around 1800. He composed devotional songs to Kali, his Chosen Ideal, which Sri Ramakrishna was fond of singing.

rasagolla (ra' sa gol' la). A sweet, popular in Bengal.

Rasmani, Rani (rās' ma nī, rā' nī). A wealthy woman of the shudra CASTE, who arranged for the building of a group of temples within a compound at DAKSHINESWAR. Of these, the one to Kali, the Rani's Chosen Ideal, is the most famous. The Rani engaged RAMKUMAR as priest for the Kali temple after its dedication in 1855, and was therefore instrumental in bringing Sri Ramakrishna to Dakshineswar. She accepted the latter as her spiritual guide.

Ravana (rā' va na). Mythological demon king of Ceylon. *See* RAMAYANA.

realization. Discovery of the reality of God through direct spiritual experience.

reincarnation. The succession of birth, death, and rebirth, which results from man's ignorance of his divinity. (Philosophically speaking, this ignorance is the mistaken identification of the Atman with the SHEATHs of body, vital principle, mind, intellect, and ego.) Man remains subject to reincarnation until he awakens spiritually and realizes his divinity in the superconscious state. Reincarnation gives him repeated opportunities, in as many lives as necessary, to manifest this divinity, or spiritual perfection, and thus to achieve IMMORTALITY.

Rig-Veda (rig′ ve′ da), spelled Rik when not followed by the word VEDA. The most ancient of the four Vedas.

Rik (rik). A special form of verse in which the RIG-VEDA is written; also the Rig-Veda itself.

rishi (ri′ shi). 1. A general term for saint or seer. 2. Any of the ancient Hindu seers of spiritual truth, to whom the knowledge of the Vedas was revealed.

Rishikesh (ri′ shi kesh′). A village about 130 miles north of Delhi, at the foot of the Himalayas. Rishikesh is frequented by holy men for the practice of spiritual disciplines.

ritual worship. *See* PUJA.

roti (ro′ tī). Same as CHAPATI.

Rudra (rud′ ra). A name of Shiva.

rudraksha (rud rāk′ sha). The kernel of the berry from a tropical tree of Asia *(Elaeocarpus ganitrus)*, commonly used as a bead in Hindu rosaries.

sadhaka (sā′ dha ka). A male spiritual aspirant.

sadhana (sā′ dha na). The practice of spiritual disciplines. *See also* AUSTERITY.

sadhika (sā′ dhi kā). A female spiritual aspirant.

sadhu (sā′ dhu). A holy man, particularly a monk.

Saguna Brahman (sa′ gu na bra′ man). Lit., "Brahman with attributes"; the personal aspect of the Godhead.

sahasrara (sa′ ha srā′ ra). The seventh and highest of the yogic CENTERS OF CONSCIOUSNESS, located in the human cerebrum. It is symbolically spoken of in Tantric terminology as the thousand-petaled lotus.

sakhya (sakh′ ya). *See* BHAKTI YOGA.

samadhi (sa mā′ dhi). 1. The superconscious state, in which man experiences his identity with the ultimate Reality. *See also* NIRBIJA, NIRVICHARA, NIRVIKALPA, SAVICHARA, SAVI-KALPA, TURIYA. 2. Absorption, the eighth limb of raja yoga, in which the mind takes on the form of the object of medita-tion. It is defined by Patanjali as a state in which "the true nature of the object shines forth, not distorted by the mind of the perceiver."

Sama Veda (sā′ ma   ve′ da). *See* VEDA.

Samhita (sam′ hi tā). *See* VEDA.

samsara (sam sā′ ra). The ceaseless cycle of birth, death, and rebirth, to which the individual man is subject as long as he remains ignorant of his identity with Brahman.

samskara (sams kā′ ra). An impression, tendency, or po-tentiality, created in the mind of an individual as a result of an action or thought. The sum total of a man's samskaras represents his character. *See also* KARMA.

samyama (sam′ ya ma). Lit., "control"; a technical term describing the process by which DHARANA, DHYANA, and SA-MADHI—the last three steps of raja yoga—are brought to bear upon an object. The mastery of samyama leads to illumination.

sanchita karma (san′ chi ta kar′ ma). The stored-up KARMA or accumulated SAMSKARAS of an individual, which he has created in previous lives and which are waiting to fructify in a future life.

sandesh (san′ desh). A sweet, popular in Bengal.

sandhya (sandh′ yā). Worship and meditation performed at dawn, noon, and sunset by orthodox Hindus.

Sankhya (sāngkh′ ya). One of the six DARSHANAS (systems of orthodox Hindu philosophy), founded by Kapila. Sankhya postulates two ultimate realities, PURUSHA and PRAKRITI. De-claring that the cause of suffering is man's identification of Purusha with Prakriti and its products, Sankhya teaches that liberation and true knowledge are attained in the supreme consciousness, where such identification ceases and Purusha is realized as existing independently in its transcendental nature. *See also* COSMIC EVOLUTION.

sannyas (san' yās). 1. The monastic life, dedicated to the practice of complete renunciation of self and the attainment of knowledge of the supreme Reality. It is the last of the four stages into which the life of an individual is divided according to Vedic teachings. *See also* ASHRAMA. 2. Initiation during which the monastic aspirant takes the final vows of renunciation; also the status of one who has taken such vows. (In the Ramakrishna Order, a minimum period of four to five years of brahmacharya is obligatory before the vows of sannyas are conferred.)

sannyasin (san' yā' sin), also sannyasi. A monk who has taken the final vows of renunciation according to Hindu rites.

sannyasini (san' yā' si nī). A nun who has taken the final vows of renunciation according to Hindu rites.

Sarada (sā' ra dā). A name of SARASVATI.

Sarada Devi (sā' ra dā de' vī), Saradamani Mukhopadhyaya, 1853-1920, wife of Sri RAMAKRISHNA, also known as the Holy Mother. Sri Sarada Devi was born in JAYRAMBATI. At the age of five she was betrothed to Sri Ramakrishna, whom she joined at Dakshineswar when she was in her late teens. Both lived lives of unbroken continence, showing the highest ideals of the householder and of the monastic ways of life. After Sri Ramakrishna's passing away, the Holy Mother stayed most of the time either at Jayrambati or at the UDBODHAN OFFICE, Calcutta. Her whole life was one of service and self-sacrifice—to her husband, to her brothers and their families, and to her spiritual children. The young disciples of Sri Ramakrishna regarded her as their own mother, and after their guru's passing looked to her for advice and encouragement. Thus VIVEKANANDA requested her blessings before undertaking his first journey to the West. Although the Holy Mother tried to hide her extraordinary spiritual gifts under the guise of a simple country woman, she is accorded worship—and was, even during her lifetime—as an incarnation of the Divine Mother. *See also* PANCHATAPA; RADHU.

Sarada Math (sā′ ra dā mat′). An order of nuns, organized in India, in 1954, in the name of Sri SARADA DEVI.

Saradananda, Swami (sā′ ra dā′ nan da), Sharat Chandra Chakravarti, 1865-1927, a monastic disciple of Sri Ramakrishna. Sharat, a cousin of Shashi (*see* RAMAKRISHNANANDA), was one of the intimate devotees who served his guru at Shyampukur and Kashipur. After Sri Ramakrishna's passing, he joined the monastery at Baranagore. In 1896, the Swami went to London to lecture on Vedanta, and subsequently to New York. He was recalled to India in 1898 to become the first Secretary of the RAMAKRISHNA MATH AND MISSION. Swami Saradananda's planning was responsible for the building of the UDBODHAN OFFICE. Working downstairs as managing editor of the UDBODHAN magazine and keeping track of the stream of devotees who came to visit Sri SARADA DEVI, he became known as "Mother's gatekeeper." He wrote the definitive biography of his guru in the *Sri Sri Ramakrishna Lilaprasanga,* which was translated from the original Bengali as *Sri Ramakrishna the Great Master.* Swami Saradananda was an example of a saint in whose life karma, bhakti, raja, and jnana yoga were perfectly harmonized.

Sarada Prasanna (sā′ ra dā pra san′ na). Boyhood name of Swami TRIGUNATITA.

Sarasvati (sa ras′ va tī). The Divine Mother as consort of Brahma, goddess of learning, and patroness of the arts and music.

sari (sā′ rī). The wearing-cloth of Hindu women.

Sat (sat). Philosophically speaking, pure Being or absolute Existence; an aspect of Brahman.

Sat-chit-ananda (sat′ chit′ ā nan′ da), also Sachchidananda. Absolute Existence, absolute Consciousness, absolute Bliss —an epithet of BRAHMAN.

Sati (sa′ tī). A form of the Divine Mother. According to Hindu mythology, Sati gave up her body in consequence of the quarrel between her father, King Daksha, and her husband, Shiva. She was reborn as Uma, or Parvati.

sattva (sat′ va). *See* GUNA.

sattvic (sāt′ vik). Pertaining to or endowed with the GUNA of sattva.

Satya yuga (sat′ ya yu′ ga), or Krita yuga. The first of the four world periods, said to comprise 1,728,000 years. *See* YUGA.

savichara samadhi (sa′ vi chā′ ra sa mā′ dhi). A term of Yoga philosophy, referring to the state of absorption in which the mind achieves identity with a subtle object of concentration, mixed with awareness of name, quality, and knowledge.

savikalpa samadhi (sa′ vi kal′ pa sa mā′ dhi). The first stage of transcendental consciousness, in which the distinction between subject and object persists. In this state the spiritual aspirant may have a mystic vision of the Personal God, with or without form.

Self. 1. The ATMAN. 2. *(l.c.)* The EGO.

Sen, Keshab Chandra (sen′, ke′ shab chan′ dra), 1838-1884. Famous Indian reformer, and leader of the BRAHMO SAMAJ. Influenced by Christianity, which he tried to introduce into the organization, he broke with Devendranath Tagore in 1868. Keshab believed himself divinely appointed to preach an interpretation of God's law which he called Navavidhan, or the New Dispensation. Contact with Sri RAMAKRISHNA, who had great affection for Keshab, taught the latter reverence for the Divine Mother. On several occasions Keshab asked Sri Ramakrishna to address his congregation.

Shaiva (shai′ va), also Shaivite. A worshiper of SHIVA.

Shaivism. A nondualistic doctrine, based on the worship of SHIVA.

Shakta (shāk′ ta). A worshiper of SHAKTI.

Shakti (shak′ ti). God as Mother of the Universe; personification of the Primal Energy, or power of Brahman. She is the dynamic aspect of the Godhead, which creates, preserves, and dissolves the universe; in relation to which Shiva represents Brahman (the transcendent Absolute, or father aspect of the Godhead). It is a Hindu belief that the grace of Shakti, the manifested power of God, is needed before the transcendent aspect of God becomes revealed.

shalagrama (shā′ la grā′ ma). A symbol of VISHNU, in the form of an oval stone bearing certain markings. A natural formation, it is found in certain riverbeds in India, especially in the Gandaki.

Shambhu (sham′ bhu). 1. Lit., "the auspicious"; a name of Shiva. 2. Shambhu Mallick, a householder-devotee of Sri Ramakrishna.

Shankara (shang′ ka ra). A name of Shiva.

Shankara (shang′ ka ra), or Shankaracharya. One of the greatest philosopher-saints of India, and chief exponent of nondualistic Vedanta. The dates assigned to him vary from the 6th to the 8th century, A.D. Shankara was born in western Malabar, South India. At the age of eight, when he renounced the world, he was thoroughly conversant with Vedic literature. During his brief life span of 32 years, he organized a system of monastic denominations which is still in existence today. His enormous literary output includes commentaries on the Vedanta Sutras, on the principal Upanishads, and on the Gita;

two major philosophical works: the *Upadeshasahasri* and the *Vivekachudamani* (the *Crest-Jewel of Discrimination*); and many poems, hymns, prayers, and minor works on Vedanta.

shanta (shān' ta). *See* BHAKTI YOGA.

shanti (shān' ti). Peace.

Sharat (sha' rat). Boyhood name of Swami SARADANANDA.

Shashi (sha' shi). Boyhood name of Swami RAMAKRISH-NANANDA.

shastra (shās' tra). 1. Sacred scripture. 2. Any scientific or legal treatise.

sheath. *See* KOSHA.

shishya (shish' ya). Pupil, disciple.

Shiva (shi' va). God in his aspect of Dissolver, one of the Hindu Trinity (*see* ISHVARA). When worshiped as the CHOSEN IDEAL, Shiva is the total Godhead, the supreme Reality. In relation to his power—the dynamic, creative mother aspect of the Godhead (called Shakti, Parvati, Kali, or Durga, etc.)—Shiva is the transcendent Absolute, or father aspect. Among his many names are Mahadeva, Rudra, Shambhu, Shankara, Ishana, Vishvanath, Kedarnath. His aniconic symbol is the LINGA. He is also represented as NATARAJA; as Lord of the Universe, riding NANDI, the bull of dharma; as the supreme yogi, seated absorbed in eternal meditation. Shiva is worshiped as the Guru of all gurus—destroyer of worldliness, giver of wisdom, and embodiment of renunciation and compassion.

Shivananda, Swami (shi' vā' nan da), Taraknath Ghoshal, a monastic disciple of Sri Ramakrishna. Tarak was born in the 1850's, and came to Dakshineswar between 1880 and 1881. He served Sri Ramakrishna at Kashipur, and after his guru's passing away joined his brother monks at Baranagore. Later he made a pilgrimage in northern India; and in 1897 he preached Vedanta in Ceylon, returning to Calcutta the following year. In 1902 he started the Varanasi Ashrama, staying there till

1907. In 1917, he came to Belur Math to take over the monastery's management. In 1922, he became the second president of the Ramakrishna Math and Mission, a post he held till his death in 1934. Swami Shivananda was known in the Ramakrishna Order as Mahapurush Maharaj (Mahapurush means "great soul")—a tribute to his spirituality.

Shiva Ratri (shi′ va   rā′ tri). An all-night vigil in early spring, dedicated to SHIVA, and observed by worship, meditation, and fasting.

shloka (shlo′ ka), also sloka. A verse. Specif., a couplet; the chief verse form of the Sanskrit epics, defined by Webster as "a distich consisting of two lines of sixteen syllables each or of four octosyllabic hemistiches."

shraddha (shrad′ dhā′). FAITH.

shraddha (shrād′ dha). A Hindu memorial service, honoring a deceased relative. It is held on the day after the period of family mourning is over and observed annually thereafter.

Shruti (shru′ ti). Scriptural teaching regarded by orthodox Hindus as directly revealed by God to man; *i.e.*, the VEDAS.

Shuddhodhana (shud′ dho′ dha na). The father of Buddha.

shudra (shū′ dra). *See* CASTE.

Shuka (shu′ ka), or Shukadeva. The narrator of the Bhagavatam and son of VYASA. Shuka is revered as one of India's greatest sages and ideal monks.

Shyama (shyā′ mā). A name of the Divine Mother KALI.

Shyampukur (shyām′ pu′ kur). A northern section of Calcutta where, in October 1885, Sri Ramakrishna moved to a house at 55 Shyampukur Street and stayed for two and a half months.

siddha (sid′ dha). 1. A perfected soul. 2. A semi-divine spirit.

Siddhartha (sid′ dhār′ ta). *See* BUDDHA.

Siddhesvari (sid' dhesh' va rī). A name of the Divine Mother, consort of Shiva.

siddhi (sid' dhi). 1. Spiritual perfection. 2. OCCULT POWER. 3. An herbal drug.

Sikhism, from sikh, lit., "disciple." The Indian religion, prevalent in the Punjab, which was founded by NANAK.

Sita (sī' tā). Consort of Sri RAMA, and daughter of King JANAKA. Sita is regarded by the Hindus as the embodiment of the ideal wife. *See also* RAMAYANA.

sitar (si tār'). A plucked stringed instrument of India, developed from the ancient VINA. Smaller than the vina, and with a straight neck, it has seven main strings and nineteen sympathetic resonating strings.

Smriti (smri' ti). Auxiliary scripture, explaining and elaborating the SHRUTI. The Smritis constitute the body of traditional law, secular as well as religious, which guides the daily life of the Hindus. They were delivered originally by Manu, Yajnavalkya, and other inspired legislators, to their respective pupils, and committed later from memory to writing.

soma (so' ma). A milk-weed, *Asclepias acida,* whose juice in Vedic times was made into a beverage and offered in sacrifices.

Sphota (spo' ta). Lit., "idea [or] sound that makes the mind burst open like a blossom"; the Logos, or sound-essence, whose symbol is OM.

Sri (shrī). 1. A name of LAKSHMI. 2. The word (which means "revered" or "holy") is used as a prefix to honor a deity, or a holy personality, or a sacred book. 3. The Hindu equivalent of the English "Mr."

Srimat (shrī' mat), or in combination, Srimad. A word which means endowed with or possessed of holiness or auspiciousness. It is used as a prefix; *e.g.,* Srimad Bhagavatam.

Srimati (shrī' ma tī). 1. A name of RADHA. 2. The Hindu

equivalent of the English "Miss" or "Mrs."

srishti (srish' ti). Projection or gradual unfoldment of what exists potentially in the cause; used with reference to the evolution of the universe from its seed state.

stages of life. *See* ASHRAMA.

Subhadra (su bha' drā). Sister of Sri Krishna. *See also* JAGANNATH.

Subodh (su' bodh'). *See* Swami SUBODHANANDA.

Subodhananda, Swami (su' bo dhā' nan da), Subodh Chandra Ghosh, 1867-1932, a monastic disciple of Sri Rama-krishna. Subodh, also called Khoka ("Baby"), came to Dak-shineswar in 1884. After his guru's passing away, the Swami went on pilgrimages in various parts of India. He worked for the Ramakrishna Math and Mission, first administering plague and famine relief, later as treasurer of the organization. His extensive tours of Bengal served to spread the message of Sri Ramakrishna. In the person of Swami Subodhananda, a child-like and unassuming simplicity was matched with the wisdom and love of the perfected saint.

subtle body. The vehicle of mind and character (linga sha-rira, in Sanskrit), which in the unillumined does not disinte-grate at death but forms the basis of a new physical body. Philosophically speaking, the subtle body consists of prana-maya-kosha, manomaya-kosha, and vijnanamaya-kosha; *see* KOSHA. It may also be considered as consisting of 17 constitu-ent parts: 5 organs of perception (sight, hearing, smell, taste, touch); 5 organs of action (tongue, hands, feet, organs of excretion and generation); 5 modifications of prana (which control breathing, digestion, etc.); mind; intellect.

Sufism. Islamic mysticism.

sushumna (su shum' nā). The hollow canal which runs through the center of the spinal cord in the human body. It is flanked on the left by the IDA and on the right by the PIN-

GALA—the main channels through which the afferent and efferent nerve currents travel. When the KUNDALINI becomes awakened in the spiritual aspirant, it passes through the CENTERS OF CONSCIOUSNESS which are located in the sushumna.

sutra (sū′ tra). Lit., "thread"; an aphorism or terse sentence into which a general doctrine or truth is compressed, usually for ease in memorizing. All the six systems of Hindu thought (*see* DARSHANA) were originally compiled in aphoristic form. The VEDANTA SUTRAS and YOGA SUTRAS are the most famous aphorisms of Hinduism.

svadhishthana chakra (svā′ dhish′ tā na chak′ ra). The second of seven yogic CENTERS OF CONSCIOUSNESS in the human body, located near the organ of reproduction.

svaha (svā′ hā), also swaha. A mantra uttered after the offering of an oblation. It means: "So be it!" or "May good come of it!"

Swami (swā′ mī). Lord, master, spiritual teacher. The word Swami, a title of the Hindu monk, may be used instead of the name or preceding the name.

Swamiji (swā′ mī jī). 1. A respectful way of addressing a Swami. 2. In the Ramakrishna Order, a term often specifically applied to Swami VIVEKANANDA.

tabla (tab′ lā). The most popular two-piece drum of India. The right-hand drum is called tabla; the left-hand drum, called baya, acts as a bass drum. Both are played simultaneously with the hands.

tamas (ta′ mas). Lit., "darkness"; *see* GUNA.

tamasic (tā′ ma sik). Pertaining to or characterized by the GUNA of tamas.

tanmatra (tan′ mā′ tra). *See* COSMIC EVOLUTION.

tanpura (tān′ pu rā). A plucked stringed musical instrument, similar in shape to the VINA but with a larger bowl made of wood or gourd. It is held upright and used as a drone.

Tantra (tan′ tra). A religious philosophy according to which SHAKTI is usually the main deity worshiped, and the universe is regarded as the divine play of Shakti and Shiva. The word Tantra also applies to any of the scriptures commonly identified with the worship of Shakti. Tantra deals primarily with spiritual practices and ritual forms of worship. The goal of these practices is liberation from ignorance and rebirth through the direct knowledge that the individual soul and the Godhead (Shiva-Shakti) are one. *See also* VAMACHARA. In addition to the Shakta Tantras there are Buddhist and Vaishnava Tantras.

tantradharak (tan′ tra dhā′ rak). One who assists the worshiper by reading instructions during the performance of a PUJA.

Tantric (tān′ trik). 1. A follower of TANTRA. 2. Pertaining to TANTRA.

tapas (ta′ pas). Penance, AUSTERITY, spiritual discipline.

tapasya (ta′ pas yā). An act or course of TAPAS.

Tara (tā′ rā). Lit., "Savior"; a name of the Divine Mother, consort of Shiva.

Tarak (tā′ rak). Boyhood name of Swami SHIVANANDA.

Tat tvam asi (tat′ tvam′ a′ si). *See* MAHAVAKYA.

Thakur (tā′ kur). Lit., "master, lord"; Sri Ramakrishna's familiar name among his devotees, often translated as "the Master" in writings on Sri Ramakrishna.

Tota Puri (to′ tā pu rī). A monk of the Shankara Order who, in 1864, initiated Sri Ramakrishna into monastic life and taught him nondualistic Vedanta.

Treta yuga (tre′ tā yu′ ga). The second of the four world periods, said to comprise 1,296,000 years. *See* YUGA.

Trigunatita, Swami (tri′ gu nā′ tī′ ta), Sarada Prasanna Mitra, 1865-1915, a monastic disciple of Sri Ramakrishna. Sarada Prasanna came to Dakshineswar in 1884, and served

Sri Ramakrishna at Kashipur. He joined the brotherhood at Baranagore, and upon taking the sannyas vows was named Trigunatitananda (shortened to Trigunatita). In 1891 he made a pilgrimage to Brindavan and in 1895 to Kailas. He became the first managing editor of the *Udbodhan* magazine. In 1902, he went to San Francisco as head of the Vedanta Society of that city, a position he held until his death. Swami Trigunatita was an austere soul and a dedicated worker. It is due to his efforts that the first Vedanta temple in the West was built.

Tukaram (tu′ kā rām). A Vaishnava saint of western India, 1568-1650, who emphasized JAPA as a spiritual practice.

tulsi (tul′ sī), also tulasi. An Indian variety of basil; its leaves are used in the worship of Vishnu.

Tulsidas (tul′ sī dās′), also Tulasidas. A Vaishnava saint and poet, 1511-1637, who composed in Hindi a Ramayana based on the original work by Valmiki. *See* RAMAYANA.

Turiya (tu rī′ ya). The superconscious; lit., "the Fourth," in relation to the three ordinary states of consciousness—waking, dreaming, and dreamless sleep—which it transcends. The Mandukya Upanishad—in which all the states of consciousness are analyzed—describes Turiya negatively, as "neither subjective nor objective experience, neither consciousness nor unconsciousness, neither knowledge of the senses, nor relative knowledge, nor inferential knowledge"; and positively, as pure unitary consciousness, ineffable peace, and as the ATMAN. *See also* NIRVANA.

Turiyananda, Swami (tu′ rī yā′ nan da), Harinath Chattopadhyaya, 1863-1922, a monastic disciple of Sri Ramakrishna, known as Hari. He came to Dakshineswar in 1884, and was regarded by his guru as the embodiment of the renunciation which is taught in the Gita. Having joined the Baranagore monastery in 1887, Swami Turiyananda subsequently made pilgrimages in northern India. In 1899, he accompanied Swami

Vivekananda to America, working first in New York, and after a brief visit to Los Angeles in San Francisco. He established the Shanti Ashrama, a retreat in the San Antonio Valley of northern California. In 1902, the Swami returned to India, dividing his time between Belur Math, Kankhal, Almora, Puri, and Varanasi. He was a deep student of the Hindu scriptures; and his purity, love, and contemplative nature inspired many to devote themselves to God.

tyagi (tyā′ gī). A man of renunciation.

Udbodhan (ud′ bo′ dhan). A Bengali magazine of the Ramakrishna Order, started in 1899. Among its first editors were Swami TRIGUNATITA and Swami SARADANANDA.

Udbodhan Office, also known as Mother's House. A house in the Baghbazar section of Calcutta, built in 1908, of which the upstairs served as residence for Sri SARADA DEVI, and the downstairs as the business establishment of the UDBODHAN magazine.

Uddhava (ud′ dha va). A disciple of Sri Krishna, to whom many of the teachings in the BHAGAVATAM are addressed.

Uma (u′ mā). *See* PARVATI.

upadhi (u pā′ dhi). Limiting adjunct; a Vedantic term referring to the bondage of ignorance which the Atman imposes upon itself by its identification with body, mind, senses, intellect, and ego.

upanayana (u′ pa na′ ya na). Investiture with the sacred thread; a ceremony during which a boy takes vows to observe purity, truthfulness, and self-restraint, and is initiated into the GAYATRI mantra. The ceremony makes him a full participant in the Hindu faith, and, thereafter, he is permitted to perform ritual worship (PUJA). In Bengal, only brahmin boys receive the sacred thread.

Upanishad (u′ pa ni′ shad). The sacred scripture which constitutes the philosophical portion of the VEDAS. The Upanishads teach the knowledge of God and record the spiritual experiences of the sages of ancient India. Of the 108 Upanishads which have been preserved, the principal ten are: Isha, Kena, Katha, Prasna, Mundaka, Mandukya, Chandogya, Brihadaranyaka, Aitareya, and Taittiriya. Since Upanishads brought to a close each of the four Vedas, they became known as the VEDANTA—the *anta* or end of the Vedas.

Uttara Mimamsa (ut' ta ra mī mām' sā). Another name of the Vedanta philosophy, written originally in the form of aphorisms and known as the VEDANTA SUTRAS; one of the six DARSHANAS (systems of orthodox Hindu thought).

vaidhi bhakti (vai' dhī bhak' ti). Preparatory devotion to God, characterized by the observance of rules and rituals—preliminary to spontaneous divine love.

Vaikuntha (vai' kun ta). Heaven; the abode of VISHNU.

vairagya (vai' rāg ya). Dispassion, renunciation.

Vaisheshika (vai' she shi' ka). One of the six DARSHANAS (systems of orthodox Hindu philosophy), compiled by Kanada. Its object is to expound virtue in order to help man unfold the highest good, attainable through immediate perception of the ultimate realities of Self and the universe.

Vaishnava (vaish' na va). A follower of the doctrine of VAISHNAVISM.

Vaishnavism. A religious sect of Hinduism, whose members follow the path of devotion to God as VISHNU or one of Vishnu's avatars—especially Sri RAMA, Sri KRISHNA, and (in Bengal) Sri CHAITANYA.

vaishya (vaish' ya). *See* CASTE.

Vallabha (val' la bha). A saintly philosopher of India, devoted to Sri Krishna, who lived during the first half of the 16th century. Vallabha wrote commentaries on the Brahma Sutras and the Bhagavatam.

Valmiki (vāl' mī ki). Hindu sage and author of the RAMA-

YANA.

vamachara (vā′ mā′ chā ra). The "left-handed" mode of TANTRA. The use of wine and women in its ritual was originally intended to teach the spiritual aspirant freedom from passions by training him to see the presence of the Divine Mother in all objects and actions, and thus to lead him gradually from enjoyment through sublimation to renunciation. When the worship degenerated into sensualism, it was outlawed.

vanaprastha (vā′ na pras′ ta). *See* ASHRAMA.

Varanasi (vā′ rā′ na sī), formerly Banaras or Benares, also known as Kashi. The sacred city on the Ganges in Uttar Pradesh, India. Its two presiding deities (VISHVANATH and ANNAPURNA) are believed to give liberation to all who die there.

Varuna (va′ ru na). A Vedic god; the presiding deity of the waters.

Vasudeva (vā′ su de′ va). A name of Sri Krishna.

Vasudeva (va′ su de′ va). The father of Sri Krishna.

vatsalya (vāt′ sal ya). *See* BHAKTI YOGA.

Veda (ve′ da). The most ancient scripture of the Hindus, regarded by the orthodox as direct divine revelation and supreme authority in all religious matters. There are four Vedas: the RIK, the Sama, the Yajur, and the Atharva—each consisting of a ritual or "work" portion and a philosophical or "knowledge" portion. Each ritual portion comprises Samhitas (a collection of mantras or hymns, most of which are addressed to deities such as Indra or Varuna); Brahmanas (which are concerned with details of sacrificial rites and with specific duties and rules of conduct); and Aranyakas (or forest treatises, which emphasize the spiritual interpretation of religious rites and ceremonies). Each knowledge portion comprises UPANISHADS. The ritual part of the Vedas is known as Karmakanda, and the philosophical part as Jnanakanda.

Vedanta (ve′ dān′ ta). Lit., "end of the Veda." A religious

philosophy which has evolved from the teachings of the latter,
or knowledge, portion of the VEDAS (the UPANISHADS). In this
sense, it is the common basis of all religious sects of India.
From the strictly philosophical standpoint, Vedanta is one of
the six DARSHANAS (systems of orthodox Hindu thought) and
based upon the VEDANTA SUTRAS, which in turn have given rise
to various interpretations (*see* VEDANTA SCHOOLS OF THOUGHT).
Through all its varied shades (dualistic, qualified nondualistic,
pluralistic, realistic, and nondualistic), Vedanta teaches that
the purpose of man's life is to realize the ultimate Reality, or
Godhead, here and now, through spiritual practice. The word
Vedanta may refer solely to the nondualistic aspect of the
philosophy, Advaita Vedanta. Advaita Vedanta declares that
the manifold universe of name and form is a misreading of
the one ultimate Reality. (This Reality is called Brahman when
regarded as transcendent, and Atman when regarded as immanent.) Since it is omnipresent, this Reality must be within
every creature and object; man, therefore, is essentially divine.
Direct superconscious experience of his identity with Atman-
Brahman releases man from all worldly bondages he has super-
imposed on his true nature, granting him spiritual perfection
and eternal peace. Vedanta accepts all the great spiritual
teachers and personal or impersonal aspects of the Godhead
worshiped by different religions, considering them as manifestations of the one Reality. By demonstrating the essential
unity at the source of all religions, Vedanta serves as a frame-
work within which all spiritual truth may be expressed. Vedanta is often, but less correctly, called Hinduism, a word
first used by the Persians for the inhabitants of India, because
they lived on the far side of the river Sindhu, or Indus. (For
Vedanta cosmology *see* COSMIC EVOLUTION.)

Vedanta schools of thought. The three main schools of
thought in VEDANTA (one or more of which are also found in

other religions) are dualism (DVAITA), qualified nondualism (VISHISHTADVAITA), and nondualism (Advaita VEDANTA). These three concepts are not mutually contradictory, but successive steps in spiritual realization—as Sri Ramakrishna pointed out —the third and last being attained when the aspirant loses all consciousness of self in union with the Godhead. To illustrate the three attitudes, Sri Ramakrishna quoted HANUMAN's words addressed to Sri Rama: "When I consider myself as a physical being, thou art the master, I am thy servant. When I consider myself as an individual being, thou art the whole, I am one of thy parts. And when I realize myself as the ATMAN, I am one with thee."

Vedanta Sutras (ve' dān' ta   sū' tras). A treatise by Vyasa on Vedanta philosophy in the form of aphorisms, interpreting and organizing the UPANISHADS. The aphorisms are also referred to as Brahma Sutras because they deal with the knowledge of Brahman.

Vedantist, also Vedantin. A follower of VEDANTA.

vidya (vid' yā). Knowledge.

vidya-maya. *See* MAYA.

Vijaya day (vi' ja yā). The last day of the DURGA PUJA, on which the image of the deity is immersed in water. The day is also observed by the exchange of greetings and good will.

vijnana (vi gñā' na). A high state of spiritual realization, or intimate knowledge of God, as a result of which the universe and all living beings are seen as manifestations of the Divine.

vijnanamaya-kosha   (vi gñā' na ma' ya ko' sha).   The sheath of intellect. *See* KOSHA.

Vijnanananda, Swami (vi gñā' nā' nan da). Hari Prasanna Chattopadhyaya, 1868-1938, a monastic disciple of Sri Ramakrishna. Hari Prasanna came to Dakshineswar in 1883. He was a district engineer in the Indian government service before he joined the brotherhood at Alambazar in 1896. The Swami supervised the construction of buildings of the Ramakrishna Math and Mission at Belur and in Varanasi; and he established a Mission center at Allahabad. In 1934, he became vice president of the Order, and in 1937, president. Swami Brahmananda, his brother monk, referred to Vijnanananda as "a hidden knower of Brahman."

vilva. *See* BEL.

vina (vī' nā). A large plucked stringed instrument of India, with a bowl-shaped body carved from a single piece of wood, and a long neck curved downward at the end with a gourd attached to the underside.

Virat (vi rāt'). The all-pervading Spirit in the form of the universe.

Vishishtadvaita (vi shish' tā dvai' ta). Qualified nondualism; a school of Hindu philosophy, founded by RAMANUJA, which teaches that all living creatures and non-living matter are parts of Brahman, who is their soul and controlling power. *See also* VEDANTA SCHOOLS OF THOUGHT.

Vishnu (vish' nu). Lit., "the all-pervading"; God as the Preserver, one of the Hindu Trinity. As the Chosen Ideal of the Vaishnavas, Vishnu represents not only the preserver aspect of ISHVARA, but Ishvara himself. Among the many forms of Vishnu, a familiar one is his four-armed aspect, in which he is seen holding a discus, a mace, a conchshell, and a lotus. Another form is the SHALAGRAMA. According to the doctrine of AVATAR, Vishnu appears on earth when needed for the good of the world.

vishuddha chakra (vi shud' dha chak' ra). The fifth of seven yogic CENTERS OF CONSCIOUSNESS in the human body.

Vishvanath (vish' va nāt). Shiva as Lord of the Universe; one of the two presiding deities of VARANASI.

Vivekananda, Swami (vi ve' kā' nan da), Narendranath
Datta, 1863-1902, monastic disciple and chief apostle of Sri
Ramakrishna. Known as Naren or Narendra (and later as
Swamiji), he came to Dakshineswar in 1881. Sri Ramakrishna
not only recognized him as one belonging to the class of
ISHVARAKOTIS, but trained him to become his message-bearer.
After Sri Ramakrishna's passing away, Swami Vivekananda
became the leader of his brother monks. He stayed for a time
at the Baranagore monastery, leaving in 1890 to practice spir-
itual disciplines in various parts of India. In 1893, he represented Hinduism at the World's Parliament of Religions in
Chicago, and subsequently held lectures and classes in various
American cities and in London. (The Vedanta Societies in the
West are a direct outcome of the Swami's visit and influence.)
Upon his return to India in 1897, Vivekananda devoted himself to the affairs of the monastic brotherhood (the Ramakrishna Math) and the founding of the Ramakrishna Mission
(of which he became the first general president). After a second trip to America and Europe (1899-1900), he returned to
India to direct the RAMAKRISHNA MATH AND MISSION in an
advisory capacity. Swami Vivekananda is generally considered
to have been the interpreter of Vedanta in this modern age.
But, more than that, he was a saint of the highest order, dedicated to the worship of God in every being.

vritti (vrit' ti). Lit., "whirlpool"; a thought-wave in the
mind.

Vyasa (vyā' sa). Lit., "one who expounds." The compiler
of the Vedas and the Vedanta Sutras, who reputedly wrote
the Mahabharata and the Bhagavatam. Vyasa was the saintly
father of SHUKA.

Yajnavalkya (yā' gña valk' ya). A saint mentioned in the
Brihadaranyaka Upanishad.

Yajur Veda (ya' jur ve' da). *See* VEDA.

yama (ya' ma). Lit., "self-control"; the first of the eight limbs of raja yoga. Consisting of various forms of ethical practices, yama includes AHIMSA, truthfulness, non-stealing, continence, and abstention from greed. It is to be practiced in thought, word, and deed.

Yamuna (yā' mu na). A Vaishnava saint of southern India, born in 953, who renounced his kingdom to become a monk. He taught self-surrender to God as the highest ideal of human life. *See also* RAMANUJA.

yantra (yan' tra). A mystic diagram used as a symbol of the Divine, especially in Tantra.

Yashoda (ya sho' dā). The foster-mother of Sri Krishna.

Yashodhara (ya sho' dha rā). The wife of Gautama Buddha.

yoga (yo' ga). The act of yoking or joining. 1. Union of the individual soul with the Godhead. 2. The method by which such union is achieved. *See* BHAKTI YOGA, JNANA YOGA, KARMA YOGA, RAJA YOGA. 3. (*cap.*) One of the six DARSHANAS (systems of orthodox Hindu philosophy), compiled by Patanjali as the YOGA SUTRAS. Yoga provides a means of attaining the highest consciousness and final release from worldly bondages by control of the thought-waves in the mind. Same as RAJA YOGA.

Yogananda, Swami (yo' gā' nan da), Yogindranath Choudhury, 1861-1899, a monastic disciple of Sri Ramakrishna, known as Jogin (also spelled Yogin). He came to Dakshineswar between 1881 and 1882, and served Sri Ramakrishna later at Shyampukur and Kashipur. After his master's passing away, he accompanied the Holy Mother to Brindavan and received initiation from her. He lived mostly in Calcutta, occasionally serving as Holy Mother's attendant. Swami Yogananda was one of six disciples whom Sri Ramakrishna regarded as ISHVARAKOTIS.

Yoga Sutras (yo' ga   sū' tras). The famous aphorisms on Yoga philosophy and practice, compiled by Patanjali probably between the 4th century B.C. and the 4th century A.D.

Yoga-Vashishtha (yo' ga vā' shish' ta). A subordinate, derivative Ramayana, whose authorship is attributed to the sage Vashishtha. The book gives instructions on how to achieve knowledge of the unchangeable Reality which exists behind the fleeting phenomena of sense life. *See* RAMAYANA.

yogi (yo' gi), also yogin. A male person who practices YOGA.

Yogin (yo' gīn). Variant of Jogin. *See* Swami YOGANANDA.

yogini (yo' gi nī). Feminine form of YOGI.

Yogin Ma. *See* JOGIN MA.

yuga (yu' ga). One of four ages into which the duration of the world is divided according to Hindu mythology. They are Satya or Krita, Treta, Dwapara, and Kali. In the first period, righteousness is predominant, but with each succeeding age virtue diminishes and evil increases. At the end of the Kali yuga (through which the world is said to be passing at present), the whole cycle begins again with Satya yuga.

OTHER VEDANTA PRESS BOOKS

I. Meditation

In the Hours of Meditation Frank Alexander. Peaceful reflections for meditation, by a Western disciple of Swami Vivekananda. 113 pages, paperback

Meditation Monks of the Ramakrishna Order. A practical guide to the theory and practice of meditation as taught by senior monks who lived in the West for many years. Subjects covered include japam, the ways to control the mind, the mantra, and the kundalini. 161 pages, paperback

Meditation According to Yoga-Vedanta Swami Siddheswarananda. From talks given to students on meditation and its practice. The author discusses the role of japa in the awakening of the kundalini, the object of meditation, and the value of the "great silence." 190 pages, paperback

The Mind and its Control Swami Budhananda. An explanation of what the mind is, and the easiest ways to control it, using the teachings of Vedanta and Yoga. 112 pages, paperback

Toward the Goal Supreme Swami Virajananda. Direct and pertinent instructions on meditation in particular and on spiritual life generally. Gives practical answers to the doubts which overwhelm spiritual aspirants. This is a personal contact with a teacher who has actually experienced what he teaches. 155 pages, paperback

II. Yoga

General

Common Sense about Yoga Swami Pavitrananda. The science of Yoga from a basic rational standpoint. Dispells some of the continuing misconceptions about Yoga. 80 pages, paperback

How to Be a Yogi Swami Abhedananda. An explanation of the philosophy, practice, and psychology of Yoga. 204 pages, hardback

Yoga and Mysticism Swami Prabhavananda. Four lectures: "Peace and Holiness," "Yoga—True and False," "Mysticism—True and False," "Know Thyself." The author differenciates between drug induced psychic experiences and authentic mystical experiences. 53 pages, paperback

Bhakti Yoga

Bhakti Yoga is widely regarded as the easiest and most natural approach to God. It is a practice that begins, continues, and ends in love.

Bhakti Yoga Swami Vivekananda. A handbook on the philosophy and practice. 113 pages, paperback

Religion of Love Swami Vivekananda. Covers different points and approaches on bhakti yoga compared to the previous title. A good follow-up text. 114 pages, paperback

Narada's Way of Divine Love: The Bhakti Sutras Swami Prabhavananda, translator. Introduction by Christopher Isherwood. Narada's Bhakti Sutras are well known in India as a scripture on love as a means of God-realization. 176 pages, hardback

Raja Yoga

Raja Yoga is the psychological or mystical way to union with God through control of the mind by concentration and meditation. A prime source for the philosophy, practice and powers of this yoga is the Yoga Aphorisms of Patanjali. Each of the following two translations has a different emphasis.

How to Know God: The Yoga Aphorisms of Patanjali Swami Prabhavananda and Christopher Isherwood, translators. The extensive commentary emphasizes aspects of Raja Yoga that are of particular value to the Westerner. Over 178,000 copies in print. 224 pages, hardback

Raja Yoga Swami Vivekananda, translator. A detailed commentary on Patanjali's complete text, with original lectures by Swami Vivekananda on Raja Yoga. 280 pages, paperback

Jnana Yoga

Jnana Yoga is the path of intellectual discrimination, the way of finding God through analysis of the real nature of phenomena. This is a difficult path, calling for tremendous powers of will and clarity of mind. But it has attracted and made saints of many who would otherwise have not embraced religion in any form.

Jnana Yoga Swami Vivekananda. Lectures on such topics as "Maya and Illusion," "God in Everything," and "The Freedom of the Soul." 399 pages, paperback

Karma Yoga

Karma Yoga is the path to God through selfless work. It is a path best suited to vigorous temperaments which feel the call to duty and service in the world of human affairs. It leads such people through the dangers of over-eagerness and undue anxiety and shows them how to find "the inaction that is in action," the calm in the midst of turmoil.

Karma Yoga Swami Vivekananda. An explanation of karma and the way to work according to yoga philosophy. 131 pages, paperback

The titles listed may be obtained from your local bookseller or by mail from Vedanta Press, 1946 Vedanta Pl., Dept. M, Hollywood, CA 90068.